FIND ME A FAMILY

HUMAN HORIZONS SERIES

FIND ME A FAMILY

The Story of Parents for Children

Hedi Argent

A CONDOR BOOK
SOUVENIR PRESS (E&A) LTD

Phototypeset in Great Britain by
Inforum Ltd, Portsmouth
Printed and bound in Great Britain by
Anchor Brendon Ltd., Tiptree

Contents

Preface

Many people have given me the material for this book and I am grateful to them. The children and the parents have been disguised and their names have been changed, but all their stories are true and I want particularly to thank them for reading the passages that concern them and giving me permission to write about them. Some stories have been amalgamated, some families appear only once and some reappear throughout the book. The reader does not have to remember who is who because each story speaks for itself, but the connections are there to be made for those who want to make them.

This book is about adoption. It is an attempt to describe how it feels to the children, the parents and the workers who become involved in special adoption – that is the adoption of children who are older or handicapped or both.

There are many text books on adoption but this is not one of them. There are several social policy issues which have a bearing on adoption but they are not discussed here. There has been a great deal of research about adoption which has influenced our work but is not quoted in this book. If any reader wants to know more about Parents for Children, our annual reports are freely available and the British Agencies for Adoption and Fostering (BAAF) has published a series of Parents for Children practice papers which can be bought through either agency. I do not aim to add to the theory behind adoption or to produce a manual on how to do it, but I do hope to share some of the experience of adoption.

I must thank the people whose ideas I have gobbled up and used in my work and in this book with barely a backward glance to their originators: people like Kay Donley, Vera Fahlberg, Claudia Jewitt, Catherine Macaskill, Jane Rowe and my colleagues at Parents for Children all of whom have taught me about adoption.

Then I want to thank Prue Chenelles, Joan Cooper, Diana Reich, Jeanette Roberts, Jane Rowe, Hilary Alton, Phillida Sawbridge and my daughters Katie and Judith for reading the various drafts and making helpfully critical comments.

I want also to express my gratitude to the management committee and the Director of Parents for Children for unstintingly giving me the time, the opportunity and the encouragement to enjoy writing this book. And I want to say a heartfelt thank you to Denise Ward for typing it over and over again and to Sue Russell and Katina Anastasi for dealing with all the administrative bits and pieces back at the office while I have been spending the long hot summer of 1983 at home.

PHOTOGRAPHS

Cover by Ingrid Darracott who has taken most of the photographs in this book.

Other acknowledgements to
Woman's Own
Woman's Realm
Southend Evening Echo
Daily Mail
Geo. Bassett & Co.
The Colour Centre, Norwich
Community Care
Glendale Studios, Tadley

1   According to James

'Where will I be at Christmas?' asked James on 1 October 1981.

On 1 October 1981 Parents for Children celebrated its fifth birthday in an unexpected way and in a way we would not have wished.

Parents for Children is an experimental adoption agency which finds families for children with special needs; children who are older or handicapped like James. James was an intelligent eight-year-old boy who was born with a cruelly disfigured face. He had to spend the first seven years of his life in hospital abandoned by parents who could not deal with his special needs which were caused by a very rare syndrome. Ascot's syndrome affects the development of the features of an unborn infant.

When James was a baby he could not close his eyes or suck or breathe easily and his hearing could not even be tested. He had to have a whole series of cosmetic operations to give him eyelids, a better working nose and outside ears and a smaller mouth. He has had to bear acute pain and chronic discomfort and he has had to come to terms with his own growing awareness of looking different. Because he is black he has also had to sort out his feelings about living with white people. And he has had to do all this without parents at his side. Without a family to whom he was precious. Without the security of having a home where he belonged. And yet James was fortunate. There was a Sister at the hospital school where he lived who became his devoted nurse and advocate. She fought for his right to lead a normal life, to go to the village school, to have friends in the community and finally to have a family of his own. Whether a child in care who needs a substitute family ever gets one depends more often than not on the imagination and determination of one worker. Medical opinion had pronounced that James was not placeable with a family. The Sister disagreed and the local authority responsible for James took up the challenge.

James was referred to Parents for Children in the autumn of 1980. We did not imagine it would be easy to find him a family and he was not ready for family life. We had to help him first to understand his own story and his need for parents and adoption. Six months later, a family with two younger girls seemed just right for James and they wanted him. He met them three times. The parents had done all they could to prepare themselves and their children for James, but the reality was different from how they thought it would be. They could not go on. It was devastating for James to have to accept that they would not have him and they suffered because they felt that they had failed him. As James said to his next parents: 'The other family just couldn't manage it.' Neither could the second, but how they tried. They had seen James' photograph and read about him when we were already working with the first family; they came back eagerly when they heard what had happened and we welcomed their interest. They knew about children like James, they foresaw the difficulties and could assess their own capabilities and limitations. They committed themselves wholeheartedly to this hurt and damaged child and he moved in with his new mother and father in July 1981.

By 1 October the family had struggled to make James their own for ten weeks and were giving up in anger. Anger, because, although they knew all there was to tell about him and had been seeing him for weeks before he moved in, James was not the child they had hoped for, been ready for, or could feel for.

If we have learnt one thing at Parents for Children, it is that, finally, only the views of the children and the parents count. Our perceptions, predictions, insights, experience and knowledge are as nothing weighed against the instinctive reactions, chemical responses and day to day living of families with children. We cannot know what will happen when this child lives with that family, because nothing in the child's previous life or in the family's will have been exactly like that. No matter how well prepared child and family are for each other, they will not know how it feels until they get together. We can enable and support only if the adoption mixture is right, and often we stand by in respectful admiration while children and parents, with incalculable effort and unending tolerance, make the most problematic placement for adoption work. But we have also had to watch helplessly while promising placements have crumbled.

So on 1 October James had to move again and I had to move him. There is no way in which anyone could ever get used to this part of adoption work and the disruption of a placement must be considered as part of the work. The agony of all those involved is different every time but no less agonising one time than another. We know, and we assure the family and reassure the child, that the failure is rarely anybody's fault; everyone has tried hard to make it work and wanted it to work, it just cannot work every time. 'But why not this time?' is the searing mute reproach from the discarded child, wounded family and immobilised worker. Home-grown families have their ups and downs and children are rejected, neglected and may even be taken away because their parents are not always given adequate help or are people who find it too hard to manage on their own. Now here are parents who can more than manage, who see themselves and have been accepted as having something to offer, and here are children who have already been injured and whom no one can bear to harm again. How do they bear it, then? Sometimes as James' family did, by becoming angry, sometimes by concentrating only on the details, the packing, the medical card, sometimes by withdrawing into indifference and sometimes, in the long term, by coming back for another child and making it work next time. There is absolutely no evidence that people who cannot become parents to one child cannot become parents to another. When it comes to moving a child there is nothing the tormented worker can do to help the tormented family, except let them do it in their own way. Far better to concentrate on the tormented child.

When I collected James I expected him to show grief and despair, and he did after the numbness had worn off and we had been driving for an hour. I also expected him to ask to go back to his hospital school, his only sanctuary. He had cried bitterly when he had to leave it. Instead he turned on me and asked accusingly: 'When will I get my real family for ever and ever?' In the midst of his own distress, James still managed to tell us that families are best for children. He celebrated our fifth birthday by confirming our belief that children need parents and upheld our faith that there are parents somewhere for every child by declaring his readiness to risk himself once more. And he did. But he still wanted to know: 'Where will I be at Christmas?' How does it feel to be eight years old and not to know where you will be next Christmas, or who with?

James stayed for a two week holiday with his hospital Sister and then he moved to an experienced family to recover and prepare for the next time. But there was no next time because these parents wanted him to become their son. He is now a fully established member of this large family with an assortment of black and white, home-grown, adopted and foster children. He goes to the village school, has many friends and is catching up with learning and with loving. It has not been easy going all the time, although his new parents have not had the problems that both of the other families worried about, or at least they did not see them as problems. And that is how one family can do what another cannot, as well as the other way round. But neither the families nor the workers can know for sure which way round it will be until it happens.

This family could accept that James was confused, attention seeking and selfish; even when they overheard him threatening his new younger brother with dire consequences should he love anyone except James and that included a prohibition on loving his Mum and Dad! They understood that he wet the bed more or less deliberately and they were wise enough to know that he was counting the days to see if he would be sent away again after ten weeks. Exactly ten weeks to the day he was drying the dishes after supper and asked in as casual a voice as only a scared eight-year-old can muster: 'Am I all right, then?' He was and is and his story contains all the hope and despair, failure and success of Parents for Children.

2   In the Beginning

We didn't have any children to place and we didn't have any families. We opened our agency on 1 October 1976 but we could not open our doors because we did not have an office. We began work in the Director's home. Phillida Sawbridge had already been in the post for a month and a great deal of her time had been taken up looking for the right premises. We did not want anything smart, but it had to be easy to find and on as many public transport routes as possible.

As we sat around that first morning, drinking cups of coffee, eyeing each other curiously and jotting down good ideas, we almost felt that we were making it all up as we went along; Phillida's skill has always been to give us scope and time and credit while guiding us in the right direction. And the direction for Parents for Children had been carefully planned.

Parents for Children was launched to test out whether every child with special needs could be adopted. Adoption is for life. It is the only method of giving a child who has lost parents a secure and legal replacement. There are other ways of caring for children who cannot live with their biological families; our brief has always been to push out the boundaries of adoption, but at the same time to monitor what parents and children need to make adoption work. Parents for Children is not the only adoption agency set up in the United Kingdom to place children with special needs, but it was the first, and it remains the only completely independent one at the time of writing, unattached to either a local authority or larger voluntary organisation. It began because the time was ripe for it.

Some social workers had been made acutely aware of the need for a special service by the findings of Jane Rowe and Lydia Lambert published in 1973. 'Children Who Wait'

5

confirmed every fear about children who live in institutions, children for whom long term plans are never made, and children who drift in and out of care with less and less likelihood of returning permanently to their own parents.

The report of the departmental 'Committee on Adoption of Children 1972' noted that the situation was beginning to change, that there were apparently families able to take a handicapped or older child and that there were far more people waiting to adopt than there were conventional babies needing parents.

No one ever envisaged that every disappointed childless couple would be able, or indeed would want, to parent an older or more complicated child, but somehow the idea of a vast untapped resource of all kinds of parents began to grow and formed the basis of a belief that somewhere there is a family for every child and that if we do not find it we have not tried hard enough. And every child began to mean not only those with 'Fit for Adoption' stamped on their medical records. All children to be adopted should be medically examined, but we do not accept that any child is unfit to have parents. A family history of mental illness, diabetes, epilepsy or tuberculosis does not mean that a child should live without a family. Even when the label 'Fit for Adoption' was no longer used, disabled children taken into care as babies and growing up in hospitals and Homes were not commonly considered adoptable. It was a major shift in attitude and concern for them to be included in an adoption society's plans, for these were the children who were traditionally left behind.

They were even left behind at the Adoption Resource Exchange. This organisation was, exactly as its name implies, an exchange service for families and children set up as a first response to the special need. Local authorities and voluntary agencies could register approved would-be adopters and hard to place children and the Exchange would match them so that a child from Surrey could be introduced to a family from Glasgow. To begin with healthy black babies were 'hard to place' but by 1975 more and more children were put forward as being in need of substitute parents and it became uncomfortably clear that the oldest, the brother and sister groups, and the most handicapped children got stuck while the younger healthier ones got placed. It seemed that if these children were not always to remain at the bottom of every pile, an agency would have to be set up which could afford not to operate a pile system. In due course the Director of the Adoption Resource Exchange, Phillida Sawbridge, became the Director of Parents for Children. At Parents for Children we have always been able to concentrate on each child until a family is found without pressure to place the easier ones first. As times change and more children with special needs are adopted, so the children referred to Parents for Children become older and more disabled.

Not only social workers wanted a new service for children. Adoptive parents and would-be adoptive parents who had been alerted to the needs of older and handicapped children, now found that many of these children were not available for adoption because they were not identified. Some local authorities denied that they had any such children in their care, others frankly admitted that it would take time to review the needs of each child with permanent family placement as a new option. The adopters would not take 'no' for an answer. Their organisation, the Parent to Parent Information on Adoption Services (P.P.I.A.S.) got together with interested social workers and began to put pressure on the government of the day to fund an independent specialist agency which would not only find families for the most hard-to-place children but provide an incentive to local authorities to consider adoption as an alternative for any child.

This pressure group, which became a steering group for our agency-to-be, and finally provided the nucleus for our management committee, drew on the growing experience of specialised adoption agencies in America. Then in 1973 Kay Donley, the Director of the agency on which Parents for Children was finally to be modelled, came to England and further electrified social workers and parents into action. She brought revolutionary common sense ideas from across the Atlantic and proved to us that they worked.

It was one of those rare occasions when the time and the place are right, when people can talk to each other and listen and when there is just enough money available to yield to pressure. The Department of Health and Social Security promised to make a substantial grant to the new agency for a three year period on the understanding that the agency would charge fees to local authorities for placing each child and would raise one third of its income by other means. Parents for Children is now in its third financial three-year period, but the basis of its funding remains the same and the element of fund-raising, worrying and time-consuming as it can be, has ensured our voluntary status and given us scope to raise money for special projects.

So we came into being with much good will and a philosophy that family living may not be right for every child, but that every child has a right to a family. We have not deviated from this philosophy over the years, but we have come to question the nature of the family.

We set out wanting to prove that every child is adoptable, but not every child we have worked with has been adopted. We were convinced that there were parents somewhere for every child but we have not always found them and when we have found them they have not always been accepted as parents for that child. We felt sure that almost everyone could be a parent, given the right circumstances, and we still believe that, although we now know that there are some people for whom we shall never have the right child.

We were three social workers, a secretary and a director, strangers to each other, but immediately thrown into a close working relationship. We were not at all sure that anyone would refer children to us. Initial publicity about the agency had not produced more than a handful of enquiries. We felt nervous about our ability to attract parents. Yet we agreed on certain basic issues in those early days and made practical decisions which set us off in the direction we still pursue.

Our first common ground was our determination to work in as open, informal and informative a way as possible with children, families, our own committee, outside agencies and each other; with special reference to avoiding the 'mixed message'. We wanted to be honest with children and did not want to sidestep their pain; we hoped we could work with parents by sharing with them what we knew and we made sure we worked closely with our adoption panel. Every adoption agency has to have an adoption panel formally to recommend the placement of each child with each family. Our panel is made up of adoptive parents and workers experienced in adoption and handicap, including a paediatrician who is our medical adviser and is available to give medical information to parents. We are also voting members but so far a vote has not been necessary. The panel supports and guides us in our work with children and families, so we do not expect it to refuse a final recommendation for a placement but we do not regard approval as automatic, for the panel has often made us think again about a need, reconsider a conclusion or go back and do some more work with a family or a child.

We have always fiercely defended the notion that families should be prepared for adoption and supported, rather than the widely accepted approach of supervision and assessment, not to mention 'vetting' and 'screening', words which in themselves are surely offensive to people who want to build families, not to enter the secret service or to win a contest. And we agreed that we would welcome single parents, divorced or re-married parents, unmarried parents and would-be parents of all ages and from all backgrounds in the belief that parents come in as many different shapes and sizes as children do.

None of us had done very much direct work with children, but we knew that they would also have to be prepared for adoption if the placements were to work. A bewildered child like James can hardly be expected to make the best of a family and a teenager who has spent much time in institutions can hardly be expected to know what a family is, however much she wants one.

Adoption is a legal process but it does not begin or end with the court hearing, and our brief not only allowed us to put time aside for continuing contact with families, it encouraged us to make the most of it. We planned to offer post-adoption support until the child comes of age as an essential part of the placement service and of our learning. It seemed unreasonable that families who were taking risks by adopting older or disabled children should be cut adrift the moment the adoption was legalised. And we knew that risk-taking would be the essence of our work.

We decided, from the beginning, that we would not work

with the birth families of the children we placed. We felt that if we were going to act as advocate for the needs of the child and the adoptive families, we could not also pursue the interests of the natural parents. We hoped that children would be referred to us only after every attempt to keep them with their birth families had failed and that natural parents would have their own local authority social worker to see them through the adoption. If natural parents are not in agreement with the adoption plan it is essential that they should have independent advice. If they support the plan it is essential that they should be able to distance themselves from their child if they wish. We have always declared our readiness to find adopters who could include their new child's original family in their lives, but so far only sisters and brothers and grandparents have kept in touch. Very few natural parents have said that they would like even to meet the adopters, but then the children we place were separated from their original parents either at birth or many years ago.

We were certain that in order to find parents for children we had to make known the need. After all, no one gets up one day and decides to adopt Harry, a fourteen-year-old Down's syndrome boy, unless, like his new single parent John, they have read about him in the morning paper. And our starting point was that we had to find parents for children and never children for people who wanted to become parents. We would be giving a service to the child and we would have to find the parents for each child in turn because no one can be a parent to just any child. It seems hardly necessary to explain how the agency got its name. Nothing else would do.

So we began work with a committee behind us, but without a base, without an image and without a reputation. We invited local authorities in Greater London and the Home Counties to refer children to us and we planned to get to know the children, to learn about their special needs and to find parents for them from within a hundred-mile radius of London. We will still consider any child referred to us from our catchment area and we still seek families who live not more than two and a half hours' travelling time from London. We fear that the right parents for some child may be outside our reach, but if we go even further afield we shall have less time for placing children. Even so, when we have been persuaded by families who live outside our area that their train service is exceptional and that they just love to meet people at railway stations, we have been glad of the extra effort if they have gone on to adopt a child.

We divided up all the local authorities in our predetermined catchment area, in alphabetical order, between the four of us. We followed up a circular letter explaining ourselves and the services we were offering with a telephone call to the Adoptions Officer, if there was one, or to the Assistant Director responsible for child care. The reception we got varied from curt dismissal to mild interest and enthusiastic welcome. Some referrals were promised and even provisionally made on the telephone. Some authorities were taken aback by the fee and we ourselves were dubious about charging so much, at that stage the equivalent of keeping a child in care for six months. Some authorities said firmly that they could do the job themselves; the most aggressive response came from a man who said, 'No sale, dearie' and put the phone down. It was our first taste of antagonism towards an all-female agency. We have placed seven children for this man's department because a keen adoption worker referred them first and argued afterwards. It only takes one determined worker to get a child placed – that is the message over and over again.

The sparse morning post was the big event of those early days and it is still one of the events which colours the day. Children are referred by post, we first see their photographs in the post and learn about them from the reports that teachers, social workers, doctors, psychiatrists and houseparents have written about them. Families may respond to publicity by letter and write to us as they proceed; some parents write blow by blow accounts of a placement as a way of getting their own thoughts in order and their feelings into perspective. As one single mother put it: '. . . excuse my rambling tirade, it is my silent scream, but everything is fine really.'

We try to strike a positive note. If people write in for a healthy white baby, we do not put them off or turn them down because we have not got any. We write instead, enthusiastically, about the children who do need parents because we presume that they have not heard of them, or we steer them towards other organisations which may be looking for families for younger and less handicapped children than we are. There is inevitably some correspondence which is censorious, outraged, or both. We try hard not to react to criticism by growing defensive. Instead we have become past mistresses at the grieved, sad reply.

Seven years ago, when the first referral actually arrived, we laughed and shouted and congratulated ourselves as though we had placed the child already. The second and third referrals followed immediately and then more. We stopped laughing and took stock. Nearly all those first children had Down's syndrome – we had certainly got them, but would we ever place them?

3   Down's Syndrome

Jill and Ben were more fortunate than Susie because they had foster parents. They were almost the same age, five months with only three days between them. Susie was already two and a half and living in a Children's Home. Parents who give birth to Down's syndrome children do not always get the best advice and services to help them keep their babies and in 1974, when Susie was born, it was still unusual for handicapped babies to be placed with foster families.

Down's syndrome is not an illness. It is a variation on the human condition; a different kind of normality. People are born that way because they have one extra chromosome and no one quite knows why that should be. The extra chromosome gives them a limited intelligence and a Mongolian kind of appearance which is why they are often referred to as 'mongols'. Unless Down's syndrome children have another disability, and some of them do have heart defects or poor sight or hearing, they are as predictable and at the same time as varied as other children. But they will make progress more slowly and they will never get as far. With encouragement and care some can learn to read and write well enough to get by socially, and if employers can afford to be creative and compassionate there are simple jobs a Down's syndrome person can do with supervision. They will never become quite independent, but can manage to live in a group home if the living is made easy. Their greatest need is for affection, security and the right kind of stimulation to help them to develop their full potential and they need it that bit more, not less, than the rest of us.

Our first three Down's syndrome babies were healthy and ready and all we had to do was to start putting our ideas into practice. We had not much experience between us of placing Down's syndrome children for adoption and we feared, just possibly, we never would get more. We felt we were starting out with the most challenging of tasks and were risking the credibility of an agency not yet established. We were, and we go on doing it in spite of our establishment. Only the risks have changed over the years.

Three of us, Hilary, Juliet and I, took on a child each and set out to get to know them and the foster families and the Children's Home. There was not very much we could do to prepare the babies for adoption before they met their new parents, but we found a great deal to do to prepare for the move. We have always asked whoever knows the baby best to write, record or just to tell us about a day in the life of the child and to include even the minutest details. From 'does she wake up crying, does she like to be changed before or after she has a drink, what and how does she drink, eat, play, sleep?' through every moment of the day and on to the bedtime routine. Making a Baby Book and putting together all they know of the baby, with photographs, weight records, the date of the first smile and the first solid food, can help foster parents and nursery nurses get ready to hand the baby on; and the Baby Book will be a most valuable gift for the new parents. Then usually people caring for the baby have wanted to know about Parents for Children and they have a right to know who we are, how we work and what we mean by parents.

We had no ideas about the kind of people who might want to become the parents of Jill and Susie and Ben. We did know where we wanted to find them. We had heard of a parents' group in Southend who, by getting together and asking, had got good services going for their Down's syndrome children: good schools, good medical provision, play centres, support systems, employment opportunities and even some special housing projects. The group welcomed the idea of including adoptive parents, although other parents of handicapped children have at times been less sympathetic to people who voluntarily shoulder the burdens which have caused them so much pain. We decided, as we still had little else to do, to mount a full scale campaign in Southend. We involved Social Services, churches, libraries, doctors' clinics and the local press. We leafleted, put up posters and gave interviews and got permission to use the children's photographs for a feature article. We organised an open meeting at the Civic Centre and all four of us stood at the door on the night and waited, chewing our nails, quite sure that only the speakers and perhaps some of the press would turn up. We had asked everyone to come and thirty people came and we were delighted. There have been many triumphs since, as well as disasters, but nothing has ever quite equalled that first moment when real people came to our first meeting and wanted to know about Jill and Susie and Ben.

Our first two families came to that meeting. Hilary and I followed on with a series of adoption classes in Southend and they never missed one. Heather and Bill Sindon already had a Down's syndrome daughter of their own and they wanted another. They felt there was nothing better and they wanted Jill. We told them about adoption and they told us about life with a Down's syndrome child. Perhaps they were our greatest inspiration. Or perhaps it was Annie and Neal Gardiner, a thoughtful, unmaterialistic couple with three bright children varying in age from one to seven with room, they assured us, for Susie to slot into the middle. It would be dull, they said, if all their children were bright in the same way. And Susie shone for them. When they went to the Children's Home to meet her, this little Down's syndrome girl, who had barely got onto her feet before, tottered towards them and put out her arms and although she could not speak they heard her say, 'Daddy' as clear as a bell. Later she learned to say 'Mummy' too. Susie seemed to have been made for her new family. She was one and a half years older than the baby, but just about the same size and at the same stage of development so that the baby remained the youngest but the two were constant companions. The four-year-old brother remained the only boy, which he rather enjoyed, and the seven-year-old sister, happy in the position of eldest, had another little one to cuddle, to tend and to organise. The parents enjoyed their 'different' child as much as they enjoyed the others and felt rewarded with a brief experience of 'twins' until the baby grew bigger and more competent while Susie, who made her own kind of progress, remained just Susie.

The Sindons already knew about it, but the Gardiners were amazed to find that because they now had a mentally handicapped daughter they were treated by many as mentally handicapped parents. They could afford to be amused, to be angry or just to ignore the offenders, but they got an idea of how it might feel to be parents who had given birth to their own handicapped children. It turned them into a family committed to fight for the rights of disabled people in general and for their daughter in particular.

The Sindons and the Gardiners are two of the most conventionally desirable and obviously acceptable families we have ever worked with. They are young and attractive and solvent. They have nice homes and the mothers do not go out to work. They are resourceful and able to look after themselves. They love children and had already proved themselves as good parents. When it was time for both families to apply to the court for an adoption order and the Guardian ad Litem was appointed from the local Social Services Department, we felt bad about poaching parents from their own doorsteps and said so. They must have children waiting locally whom they could have placed with these two lovely families, we suggested. They had the children of course, only the Guardian ad Litem assured us, sadly, that although she was wholeheartedly recommending both adoptions, these were not families which their own adoption panel could approve. After all, one of them already had a handicapped child: was it normal to want another? While the other family (and was this even worse or better?) was breaking all the rules by putting a handicapped child among normal brothers and sisters and not even as the youngest! Would any family have been right, we wondered? But there is progress. This same local authority now operates its own Home Finding Unit and in 1981 we had a jubilant telephone call from the Sindons. 'Guess what', said Heather, 'we've just got our third daughter.' The Home Finding Unit had placed June, a four-month-old Down's syndrome baby.

And what of our own progress? It took longer to find parents for Ben and we did not get it right first time. Infant boys have always been harder to place than girls and the same is true for Down's syndrome babies. Ben lingered while Jill and Susie settled in with their new families. Then parents came to see us who knew what they wanted. They had fostered an older Down's syndrome girl and now they wanted to adopt a Down's syndrome baby. They would have liked a girl but we were looking for parents for Ben and they decided that as biological parents cannot choose the sex of their child neither would they. We should have persuaded them to wait to have a girl because that is what they did in the end. They worked hard to prepare themselves for Ben, they took Ben and they tried to love him but they found him unlovable, and it nearly destroyed them to say so and let him go. He went on to a childless couple who idolised him, but who in turn could not absorb an older Down's syndrome girl into their family when we placed her eighteen months later. Only then could they feel compassion as well as gratitude towards the first family which had rejected their son. Later we placed a Down's syndrome baby girl with this family and they are the splendid adopters they wanted to be and we hoped they could be.

There have been many Down's syndrome children since Ben. We have learnt that although Down's syndrome babies are usually placid and move without much fuss, they may withdraw into themselves and become depressed. Louise, aged one, went to experienced parents and was a much wanted second child. She seemed to take to Jean and Dick Johnson almost immediately and settled in without a problem. Only weeks later and slowly did Jean and Dick realise that she had cut herself off. She would always try to get into a corner of any room she was in. She would allow herself to be cuddled but did not cuddle back. She would sit for hours and pull faces and neglect her toys. And worst of all, although her face would pucker she would not cry. It took patient, loving and almost constant attention to bring Louise back. This same family taught us another and even sadder lesson.

Jean and Dick's first adopted daughter is also a Down's syndrome child. We placed Diane aged four with them from a residential nursery, with up-to-date medical reports which mentioned a slight heart murmur. The new parents were not quite happy with Diane's health and took her to see a paediatrician for an overall assessment. He diagnosed a severe heart condition, too severe to operate then, but if Jean and Dick could have had her three years earlier she could have had life saving treatment in time. Diane has failed to thrive and only survives in defiance of every medical prognosis because she has devoted parents who offer her a life worth living although they know that she will not grow up. They are bitter about the way their daughter has been neglected but 'it wouldn't have made any difference,' said Jean, 'we'd just like to have known before so we could have prepared ourselves.' They are filling every moment of her life with love and care and that includes firm discipline and normal family activities as well as compensation for what Diane has lost and will never have. We have never again placed a Down's syndrome child without a proper cardiac assessment, and we feel awed by Jean and Dick's commitment to a child who was placed in good faith, but with bad information.

There have been some funny incidents when Down's syndrome children have joined a family. A Health Visitor called on new parents after getting our notification of placement, only she had not had time to read it all. So when she looked at the baby in the pram her face expressed horror and she said to the proud mother and father: 'Do you know you've got a little mongol?' The Gardiners met a well-meaning friend who said: 'I don't suppose Susie is really a mongrel so don't worry about it,' and an acquaintance said to the Sindons: 'I expect they'll both grow out of it in time.' But no one thought it was funny when a woman accosted Annie in a supermarket and accused her of trying to get rid of her baby and now look at her! Or when a single parent consulted a doctor about her baby's persistent cough following a cold and he said to her: 'What can you expect, she's only a mongol.' Later, another doctor said to a mother: 'He doesn't need an injection for whooping cough, he's brain damaged already.' Not a very kind or humorous way to explain that the risk for Down's syndrome children could be greater from the vaccine than from whooping cough. But by no means all professionals or people in the street are ignorant about mental retardation or unsympathetic when children behave oddly or look unusual. Jean said about becoming parents to two Down's syndrome children: 'Since we've had Diane I've made an awful lot of friends, I've met an awful lot of people that speak to me now who didn't bother before.'

Nearly seven years on, placing Down's syndrome babies is not the great challenge it was. It is not hard to find families for them and nowadays we take on one at a time alongside our other work. We have placed Down's syndrome babies with single parents, with large families and with childless couples. We have placed them with families which do not put much value on achievement and we have placed them with families which can tolerate a wide variety of abilities. We have placed them with families which remain undisturbed by public opinion and reaction and we have placed one with a family who created a national stir when a seaside hotel refused their booking because they came with two Down's syndrome sons. We have placed with parents who accept Down's syndrome children as normal and parents who work to make their Down's syndrome children more normal.

There is no ideal family for Down's syndrome babies but there are families just right for Susie and Jill and Ben. There are families which had never thought of having a Down's syndrome child, until they heard of their daughter or son and there are families like Jean and Dick who have adopted Diane and Louise. They had been turned down as adopters by one agency after another. Dick was already a grandfather and Jean, thirty years younger, had spent her childhood in care. She explained why they wanted to adopt a Down's syndrome child: 'They're such lovable, affectionate children and they give you much more than you give them. They're such fulfilling and rewarding children, more so than ordinary children.' Jean and Dick did not fit a pattern; what they had to offer was not only eccentric but also exactly met the needs of their adopted children. There has been more than progress, there has been a revolution. Permanent family placement is now the first choice for every Down's syndrome baby unable to remain with its own parents and most of them will be adopted. As long as they are placed when they are babies. For Down's syndrome children, as for all children needing substitute parents, age is the biggest handicap.

4 Something and Chips – Working with Older Children

We eat while we work but we also work while we eat. Much of our work with children centres around a meal bought, prepared and eaten together. We are inclined to invite families for lunch, if they have had a long journey to London, and we readily offer bread and cheese to other colleagues. We have never analysed our preoccupation with food satisfactorily, but it clearly has to do with sharing and nurturing and an awareness of the children's unfulfilled primary needs and our own very fulfilling working conditions. We are not extravagant, we buy cheaply and simply and only when things are getting bad do we bring in cake to have with our coffee. That still leaves scope for our favourite cry for help: 'Things are getting worse, send chocolate.'

When the older children come to our office to work with us and eat with us, then no matter whether it is lunch or tea it is something and chips. Chicken and chips heads the children's list and it heads ours because it comes in handy boxes with plastic cutlery and then there is no washing up. On the other hand, washing up together can be a useful activity and James, who always had his chips with sausages and baked beans, would become shyly confidential over the dishes.

But who are these older children and why do they come to the office and what do we mean when we say 'to work'? They are all children who cannot live with their biological parents. They are children who have had 'careers' in care. They are children the local authority has decided should be adopted, but has been unable to place. They are not at the centre of a tug of love, they are not being snatched from parents who want them or from young women who should be enabled to keep them, but they have had a variety of experiences which we do not think children should have. They have all been rejected. Many have witnessed violence, some have been assaulted, they may have lived with sick families or with families falling apart around them or never have lived with families at all. They have spent most of their lives in Children's Homes and they may be anything from nine to fifteen years old by the time they come to us. They are children whose education in life does not help them to do their best; some go to special schools because they are slow learners and some have learning difficulties. The rest are usually labelled as under-achievers.

When children grow up without families they do not grow up in the same way as children who have families. Of course, each family is different and will bring up their children differently from all other families, but they will all be family children. All Children's Homes are different too and each one will treat its children differently, but they will all be Homes children whether they live in small groups or in a large institution. Not that all family life is always better than any life in care. Hardly anything is ever a totally good or a totally bad experience. Family children suffer all the inconveniences of being brought up by less than perfect parents and may end up in a big mess. Homes children need not be emotionally deprived and can be jolly, lively, energetic and all the other things that children are. Or at least they can be if placed purposefully with clear aims and careful monitoring. Unfortunately the children who come our way have not been placed in residential care by choice or as part of a treatment plan, but because there was no alternative. And few of them have been lucky enough to live in only one Home.

A child in a family has the best chance of being nurtured as a baby and protected as a toddler; of sharing in the life style of that family, learning to give, take and trust and being offered certain values and standards; being given an increasing amount of responsibility and finally guided towards independence with enough space for rebellion. Not every child in a family gets everything, but most get enough, even if the quality of it is varied and it is not always consistent.

The child in a Home is not handled by a constant group of people. Staff must change, staff must go off duty, staff must have holidays. The very small child cannot feel satisfied or safe and will find it hard to trust. It will not share the house-parents' life style for they have their own homes elsewhere. Giving and taking will be concerned mainly with material things and there will be more and more taking. Values and standards will be impersonal and may not be very meaningful. Responsibility could be regarded as unwelcome and independence as frightening, because it will threaten to come abruptly and technically when the child is eighteen. Rebellion, a healthy part of normal adolescent behaviour, may either be carefully hidden or turn into delinquency. These children become institutionalised. When children move from Homes to families they have to make tremendous adjustments and so do the families. Much of the preparation for adoption has to do with making these adjustments.

It is demanding to live in a family and to be expected to relate to parents and sisters and brothers. Parents want to know what happened at school, what is liked and not liked, what was funny and what a friend's mother said when the child went to tea. Parents are concerned about a sore throat, about a lack of appetite, about a miserable face; they are pleased by acts of kindness and achievements of all sizes but they can also be disappointed and hurt for surprising reasons. They remember dental appointments and what is promised from one day to the next and there is no escaping them because they are always there. Brothers and sisters are limited in number and permanent. It is not easy to ignore one of them for any length of time or to bully a little one without discovery. All families have their own rules about how things should be done, what can be said and what is allowed and what is forbidden; biological children grow up with the rules, but adopted children have to learn them and their individual experiences have not prepared them for making positive relationships or for learning.

There is a wealth of stories about what such children have done and said. Joan put a shop steak and kidney pie to heat up in the oven with all its wrappers on; she had never helped to cook in her Children's Home which had many cottages and a central kitchen. Selwyn was outraged when he found dust on the mantelpiece and asked when the domestic was coming.

Later he accused his new mother of neglect when he was left in a room on his own to watch television while she made the tea. And later still he made their first holiday together hell because he could not understand that it was her holiday too; staff are paid to look after the children on holiday and then go off to have holidays of their own to recover. Edward, nearly sixteen, said with glee when a younger member was about to be added to the family: 'I'll be like staff,' and Laura, when asked by another child to play 'Mummies and Daddies' was overheard saying: 'All right, you be on day shift and I'll be on nights.' Children frequently threaten their new parents with 'I'll tell my social worker of you' and they demand sweets and toys and clothes as proof of their worth. Sometimes the proof bowls them over. Nick asked and asked for a jacket which he did not really need. Finally his parents took him to buy one but insisted on the best quality so that it would last. Nick dared to put the question that is usually left unspoken, 'Am I worth that much?' But Marion cannot be persuaded of her own worth although she has been with her family for four years now and will never put her worth to the test. She will not ask for anything and her parents understand that damaged children cannot give, but that children who are more damaged cannot take because somewhere deep inside they have given up. Edward may think he will feel like staff when he has a younger brother, but he is afraid to go out on his own and he does not want to have his sixteenth birthday looming. He was separated from his natural mother when he was five years old and he has got emotionally stuck at that age. Just as he should be rebelling in safety against the solid framework of his upbringing, he must try and catch up with eleven years of family life in the hope that it is better to have it late than never.

All these children share a communication problem. In order to be able to comprehend words about families we first have to help them to construct the language. Otherwise it is like trying to learn Chinese without even perceiving that the language has a different structure from other languages we know. Children who have never seen parents working, sleeping, loving and arguing, being happy and sad, being energetic one day and tired the next, having a lazy Sunday, not enough money, worries about jobs, sick relatives, aged grandparents and new babies, how can they grasp the words to describe it? And if they do have memories of family life, it is likely to be of an unsafe and unsatisfying experience ending in loss.

All children, as they grow in awareness, have to define their own positions within as well as outside the family. If children have lost a family and are not sure who they are and why they are where they are it is hard to learn to tell the time, to find their way and to remember which day of the week it is, which month and even which year. In order to place themselves in space and time they have to find out who they are and how they got there. If children in care are confused it is because their lives have been confusing, and if they are disturbed it is because their circumstances are disturbing.

Keith was eleven and attended a remedial class at a comprehensive school. He was said to have a low borderline normal IQ but he could not learn to read and write, he was withdrawn, disorientated and described as an inveterate liar. He could certainly not tell truth from fantasy, he could not grasp the concepts of time and space and he could not make friends. Keith had been born with a tumour which was removed successfully at birth, but his inexperienced mother was so anxious about him that she always kept him safe in a cot. When he was five, first his grandmother who lived with them, and then his mother, died within weeks of each other and left him alone and still in his cot. His father was unknown. His grandmother had been a heavy diabetic woman with only one leg. His mother had nursed her and then collapsed herself. Keith could hardly walk when he was found. An aunt tried to look after him but became ill too. Two years later he was fostered but that did not last long. Keith was living in his second Children's Home and the Head of the Home was just leaving.

Keith learned about himself when he came to Parents for Children, and as he put his story together, he put himself into it. He began with the birth certificate. Keith had never heard of birth certificates, but, what mattered more, he had never known that his mother's name was Violet May. He loved that name, he was overwhelmed by the beauty of that name as he repeated it over and over again, and he treasured it on a scrap of paper that he carried around in his trouser pocket. He remembered then that his mother used to go out to buy him sweets and he could believe that she loved him. He had never liked to ask what had happened when she was carried off in an ambulance but he asked now. No one had told him that his mother had died. Of course he knew she was dead, other people had referred to her as dead, but no one had told him when she died. He had suffered her loss but had not been helped to mourn for her. Now his social worker took Keith to see his mother's grave. It was hard to find because it was a common grave. Violet May lay buried with others whose death had become the business of the council. The grave was marked with a number and there were names and that was all. On that day Keith promised himself that when he grew up he would save to buy a headstone for his mother. We cried when he told us, but surely it is more wholesome to want to buy a gravestone for a dead mother than to be adrift in a mystery about her death? When Keith had worked through from his birth certificate to his mother's death certificate he suddenly had a curious insight. For the first time he knew what his birthday was. It had never been explained to him that it celebrated his own birth and he hadn't noticed that it was always on 11 July because days and months meant nothing to him. He had thought, in a vague sort of way, that birthdays were having turns at having parties.

Keith remembered his foster parents. He liked them and thought he was staying with them forever. But one day he was in a temper and said he did not like them any more and wanted to go back to the Children's Home. He thinks that is why they packed his things and sent him back. Only first they had to get him down from the top of a cupboard where he often sat and no one knew why or how he got up there. Keith said that when he was on top of the cupboard he thought of knives and killing and was very scared.

When Keith was introduced to his new family, he was so anxious to make them his, that he called them 'Mum and Dad' as soon as he met them. Not to their face, but when he came rushing upstairs at Parents for Children to tell us that they had arrived back from their first outing together and were thirsty. 'My Mum and Dad,' he said with bursting pride and fearful trepidation, 'would like a cup of tea', and he looked as though he could hardly believe his own voice and words.

Keith was mystified by his past and thrown into confusion in the present but Sandra, aged thirteen, was filled with hate for all she knew of her past and the hatred took over the present and threatened all her future. Sandra had been treated with well-meaning honesty. She was told that she was abandoned as a baby and it was hinted that her mother was kept by men and known that her father went to prison and then disappeared. Sandra told her own story with relish and defiance. Only she believed that being abandoned meant that she was stuffed into a dustbin with the lid on. She was sure that her mother was a prostitute and her father a hardened criminal. We had to go right back to the people who found her and knew her mother and could trace her father. And then we had to repeat the story we pieced together. Sandra asked me to write it and then she wrote it. She tape-recorded it, she asked for it to be typed, and finally she pasted it into a book together with all the other bits of information she had gathered about her life.

Sandra had not been stuffed into a dustbin but had been left in a nightclub wrapped in blankets with a bottle for her next feed. Her mother was still a schoolgirl who had run away from an unkind family and, in order to earn enough money to pay for her furnished room, she was working in a nightclub as a hostess. Sandra's father was not a hardened criminal, but a young man from another country who was a stranger to English laws and got himself into trouble and was deported. He had written a letter to ask if Sandra could go back with him to his own land, and her mother had written to say that she hoped Sandra would be adopted. We found a social worker who had known Sandra's mother and she could tell Sandra that her lovely eyes were just like her mother's. Children should know what they have inherited from their natural parents and that their nose, the way their hair curls, or their voice are good gifts which can never be taken away. Sandra became confident enough when she had her story straight to ask about her natural parents now. Nothing is known of her father, but her mother has made a new life in the old area. Sandra was angry when she heard that, she wished her ill, but after a week she said that if she bothered to look for her when she was grown up she would take her a tablecloth because tablecloths make a place look nicer, don't they? It wasn't her mother's fault, she said, that when she was little she hadn't been placed for adoption and that her long-term foster placement had broken down.

Putting the past together and into a meaningful perspective is only a beginning and will not be enough to enable the child to accept the present and to look positively towards the future. The hurt and the deprivation will not go away, but Sandra may be able to grieve for what she has lost and make sense of what has been in order to absorb it and to take it along with her wherever she goes. Because if she is to be a whole person, she cannot leave bits of herself behind, not even the bits she hates.

When we began to work with older children we supposed that each child would make a life story book to hold the past, that we would prepare them for the future and act as a bridge between the two. Predictably the work with every child has been as unique as every child is and what has engrossed one child has bored another.

We tell each child about the agency, the other children and the way we will work together and we make it quite clear that the visits to Parents for Children will not be treats. Some children have been eager to work and some reluctant, but all of them have liked coming to the office. It is perhaps the most concentrated one-to-one attention they have had. They are brought and taken back by their houseparent or social worker who knows them best and there is great value in the chats before and after the session. Sometimes the Parents for Children worker will work directly with the child and sometimes she will co-ordinate the work which the houseparent does with the child. Sometimes the sessions will be weekly and sometimes monthly. Sometimes we will make a contract for six sessions and sometimes we will leave the arrangements open-ended but the child always knows what will happen next.

Broadly speaking we have not lost sight of our three themes, the past, the future and the bridge, but the nature of the work has changed, diversified and been enriched by the children. Dawn taught us how to help her to put her many chaotic uprooted memories into order. Eleven years of things remembered and pushed aside were sorted out into eleven links of a chain joined up to make her lifespan. With an uncanny instinct for self preservation Dawn had stored in her memory all the minutiae of her childhood, because there was no one else to remember for her. But by now it was hopelessly muddled and she had to unravel it and separate it out into the years of her life.

It was Dawn who also offered us a new look at rules. She liked to finish off each work session with a game of draughts. She played well and could win, but if she thought she was not going to win she cheated. We talked about rules: playing by the rules, evading them and breaking them and how families would also make rules. She was thoughtful but went on cheating. After a few weeks she preferred Snakes and Ladders and played the same way. One day she said, 'I want us to go up the snakes and down the ladders', so we did and she did not cheat, but won. Afterwards she said, 'You see, you can get the rules changed.' Whenever we played after that we went up the snakes and down the ladders and sometimes I won and sometimes Dawn won but she never cheated again because she was more interested in making the rules work than in winning.

Danny was not interested in anything, though he dutifully got himself to the Parents for Children office and waited for his tea. However he must have heard something, because when he was eighteen he asked his adoptive parents to contact us and to say that he was ready to hear it again.

Hannah's life story was unfurled slowly on a roll of wallpaper, Edward made a complex chart of the houses, people, schools and social workers he had known, Doris made lists about the sort of person she was, what she wanted out of life, expected from a family, remembered, longed for and finally a very short list of what she was willing to offer. Barbara liked to act out family situations and sometimes she was the child meeting new parents and sometimes she was the mother and I was the child she did not want to have. Oliver put everything he wanted to say on a series of steps sometimes going up and sometimes down, and Angela wrote stories and drew pictures about a girl called Avril and all the dreadful adventures she had. Mickey did not do anything at all, but he noticed what other children had done.

Even mentally handicapped children can work to prepare for family life and show us what they need and what they fear. Thelma was fourteen years old and severely retarded. She liked to play with the miniature family in the dolls' house but regularly threw the baby out of the window. If we hid the baby she made another out of pipe cleaners and threw that out. We took the hint and she did not go to the single mother with baby who had expressed interest in Thelma. Trevor could not talk about his sad frightening life – but he manipulated train crashes week after week until he became more trusting and then the two model trains went round and round on the track skilfully avoiding collision.

Harry, the fourteen-year-old Down's syndrome boy, asked Hilary, who was working with him, to draw houses with rooms and people. One day Hilary drew a large bedroom, a small bedroom and asked Harry who should sleep in the big double bed. 'Dad', said Harry without hesitation. 'Who else?' asked Hilary. 'Me', said Harry. 'Oh I think you should sleep in the little bed in the small bedroom', suggested Hilary, 'and Mum should sleep with Dad.' 'That's rude!' said Harry and he never budged from that. In all her work with Harry, Hilary could never persuade him to consider a Mum as anything but a 'cooker'. Harry had not had much going for him in his life so far but from this point on it was pure wish fulfilment. John turned up: a single man with a home of his own and a mother who comes in to cook for him; with a dog, a garden, an interest in football and a job where Harry would always be welcome to come in and help. Harry is happy with his single bedroom, content that he need not worry about anyone else taking his place with Dad.

Some children in care have more traditional desires. Tony was five, the oldest of three, and he was just losing his milk teeth. He had expected the fairies to leave a silver coin under his pillow when he lost the first one in the Children's Home and was upset when they did not. So were the residential workers who were particularly fond of Tony. Each worker had felt sure that one of the others would leave a coin. Next time round they were determined not to forget. So, when Tony lost his second tooth one member of staff put a larger than usual coin under the lefthand side of the pillow and later another left an even larger one under the right corner. Tony was almost as upset, and wanted to know if the new parents on the farm would arrange with the fairies to get it right: one silver coin for one tooth. Dawn's request was even simpler. She loved cookery at school but pretended not to because in the Children's Home they were nearly always too busy to get her the right ingredients. So she said she did not care, but she also said she wanted a mother who would never forget the swiss roll for the trifle.

Working with children who have been hurt, hurts us if we do it properly. If we avoid the painful issues we do more damage, because children will feel that they themselves are dangerous. All children need help to negotiate their place in the community and children who will be adopted need it more. But we must not let working with children become an end in itself and let ourselves be seduced into feeling we are significant people in the children's lives. We will see them at most for a couple of hours a week; it is parents who will have to live with them. We cannot be sure whether and when children are ready to make new relationships, we can only do what is necessary to help them move. No more. We may be able to explore the way, to provide that bridge from one life to the other, but it is the parents and the children who make the real beginning, who keep on going and build a family. We just go on eating chips.

5 Nothing Up Our Sleeves –
The Way We Work

We have always considered it essential to be seen to be doing
what we do, both because of a natural inclination towards
openness and because as a pioneering agency, we must be
prepared for scrutiny. If our work is to have any significance in
the area of planning for children in care, then it has to be
accessible to others. To hide our beliefs and practice and our
experience of what has worked and what has not, would seem
to us to be an abuse of the privileged position we enjoy.
Privileged, not because it is exalted, but because among social
workers there are few who can do the job they set out to do
without administrative and political pressures and with time,
support and adequate resources on their side.

In order to show what we do, we have leaflets which clearly
set out the agency's aims and methods with photographs and
potted histories of the staff. We describe the kind of children
we have placed, we encourage everybody to consider themselves as potential parents and we specify every aspect of the
service we are able to give. We make no secret of the way the
money comes and goes. We write an annual report which
keeps abreast of the story so far. We take every opportunity to
inform social workers in particular and the world in general
that we are here and how we work. We invite parents-to-be
and children to be adopted to get to know all of us and we
share with them the whole process of family finding, preparation, introductions and placement. Yet more often than
makes us comfortable, a fellow social worker will read
through everything we have produced and listen to everything
we have to say and still ask, even if not in as many words '. . .
and now tell us what you really do'. As though there were
some secret formula we were, after all, withholding. As

though we had developed skills we were concealing or even as though we were not quite abiding by the adoption rules.

Families too, have occasionally said to us that it cannot be as simple as all that. We hope they mean that they are pleasantly surprised that we are not putting difficulties in their way, but at least one couple was convinced that we hide all the children upstairs until Mr and Mrs Right come along and they would not believe otherwise in spite of our protestations and offers to show them round. They went away and did not come back and may still suffer from a sense of injustice because they were not taken to where the children really are.

When I showed the first draft of this book to a friend she also wondered what I was not telling. But it is all here, as I see it, the true story with nothing up our sleeves.

We operate from a High Street in North West London densely packed with aromatic oriental delights, continental delicacies, native health food, international fish, a riot of fruit in the market and every kind of Take Away. We work in a crumbling shop-cum-house-cum-office on three floors which we found just in time exactly where we wanted to be. We have been assured that the structure is sound, but it has an air of decay nevertheless. The shop was on the ground floor where we now have armchairs and a coffee table and books for children, about children and about adoption. We try to make it a cheerful and convenient place. We use the shop windows to display information about the agency; but they are very large windows and it is hard to keep the heat in and the noise out. There is a minute, but well used kitchen, and a lavatory with rails for disabled visitors, but a door too narrow for a wheelchair.

The middle of the house is the centre of Parents for Children. The two secretaries have the largest room and in it is every record of every meeting, every interview, every visit, and every placement. Adoption agencies have by law to keep adoption records for seventy-five years and now and again we say we must have more space because the files will take over.

Next to the main office is a small room of all trades. It is the quietest room in the house and is known as the 'interview room'. But it is also a play room. We have an unplanned mixture of toys, mostly given, which children use while their parents work with us and we use when we work with children. There are board games, building bricks, cars and dolls; two life-size bears sit on the floor and a dolls' house has pride of place and is in everyone's way simply because there is nowhere else to put it. A much valued fort made for us by unemployed school leavers and a train set have to be stowed away in the basement when not needed, because, like the files, the toys are in danger of taking over. This same small room also has a settee that opens out into a double bed so that it becomes a spare room for families who need to stay in London for introductions or who need to come long distances for hospital visits. While the parents sleep on the opened out bed which practically fills the room, their children sleep on camp beds at night in the spaces in which we work during the day. Families have decorated their spare room with pertinent posters. There is a copy of the 'Children's Charter', an agreeable print of a primitive painting, a picture of ducks who prophetically say that they have to get their feet wet in order to swim and photographs of children of different races. But we like best the poster of four owls sitting on a rafter. Our visitors have fun working out which owl is supposed to be which one of us and the similarities we are told, are plain to see, even if everyone sees them differently.

The social workers are at the top of the stairs. Phillida has a room even smaller than the interview room and from her window she has been able to watch the art-deco emergence of TV AM out of a derelict garage. We other three share the only remaining room in the house. Our offices are not spartan. They are carpeted and comfortably furnished and colourful. We are mindful of the fact that children want to see where we work and we do not want to depress them with bare rooms and forbidding desks, nor do we want to depress ourselves.

Everything around us is yellow and brown, it has become the house style; everything: the wallpaper and the paint, the furniture and the carpets, the children's posters and the writing paper. It just happened that way. We wanted to have a motif logo but we did not like any that were suggested and could not think of a better one. Then it happened. 'Let's not have a logo,' we said, 'let's have colours.' Yellow and brown it became, and we have stuck with it and sometimes we have felt stuck with it. But it had the desired effect. A lot of people know that anything on yellow paper is likely to be from us. Even Keith knew when he saw it on his teacher's desk. It was a letter about his adoption. He read it straight through to his teacher who showed surprise and said: 'Keith I've never heard you read before,' and Keith answered, 'I've never had anything to read before.'

We work hard. What pressure there is comes from each other. To get the children placed. We place children with permanent substitute families and that nearly always means for adoption. We carry small case loads. We work with only three new children and between three and five new families each at any one time. But clearly we have an ever increasing number of adoptive families to support who at times need very little from us and at other times need much more.

We place twelve children a year on average. Not many, but the number is a true measure of how long it takes and a fair indication for other agencies which want to allocate time to place children like James and Keith, teenagers like Nick and Edward, girls nearing adolescence like Sandra and Dawn, disabled children like Harry and Thelma and multiply handicapped children growing up in hospitals and institutions.

We work as a team and the team both controls and withstands the pressure. Otherwise we might rush into a placement because the child's longing is hard to hold or because a family's impatience is infectious. On the other hand the team stops any one of us from looking for ideal parents because it can happen when we become involved with a child that no family is good enough. We do not necessarily agree with each other, but we do understand what each other is saying and we have nearly always been able to go on talking until a solution acceptable to us all has been negotiated. I am an obstinate kind of person, but I have found it easy and safe to change my mind within the team and have never felt pushed to justify a viewpoint for the sake of being right. Teamwork has helped us all to avoid entrenched positions and to welcome every opinion with as little prejudice as possible. We are a small team and although we are far from thinking that small is beautiful, we do think that it is functional and comfortable; we hope it will never become comfortable enough to be cosy, but in any case the nature of the work does not make for cosiness.

We have tried to build in for ourselves the 'flexibility factor'. We hope never to stick to any rule, practice, habit, preference or even decision, if we can see or be shown a better way to deal with a particular set of circumstances. We have at times therefore been able to make changes, create new projects and become more efficient with the minimum of fuss and delay. But at other times we have not been able to bend sufficiently to make working with us easy. At yet other times we have bent too far and lost our balance. We have a saying that we are so flexible we can hardly stand up – but this is not how most of our colleagues see us, we are told.

We have been described as 'four powerful women' but we are six. First there was Lin who was joined by Helen, then there were Annie and Sue, followed by Sharon and Sheridan and now we have another Sue and Katina. Our two secretaries are the front line of Parents for Children. They know each family, every child, all the social workers involved from the many local authorities we work with and they participate in all we do. They are members of the team and they are the first to pat us on the back when something has gone well or to commiserate when it has not. These women also organise the office, the coffee and the loo paper and deal with our heavy typing demands with amazing promptness. It is not their job to make the coffee, to do the washing up or the shopping, and if they do it more often than the rest of us it is because they are more often in the office. They are the only members of staff who have come and gone on to better things and we are grateful for the time and service they have given to Parents for Children. Powerful or otherwise we could not operate without them.

Recently a colleague asked whether the rest of us came as a package or were we 'chosen' – an appropriate question to put to adoption workers. It is perhaps correct to say that we were a chosen package. Phillida Sawbridge was appointed as Director of the agency-to-be in April 1976. She came from a background rich in adoption and child care including first hand knowledge of practice in America. She brought with her a talent for languages, a half transatlantic heredity, an ability to write vigorous informative English, the experience of having lived and worked in other parts of Europe and an enabling spirit which set out to form and lead a democratic team. Hilary, Juliet and I were among the short-listed applicants who were invited to lunch with Phillida and the adoptive parents on the new management committee. That lunch became fixed in the agency's history for ever because at our formal interview we each had to remember where we had sat at table and draw a diagram to show which of our fellow guests we would most like to be our fellow workers. It would appear that Hilary, Juliet and I chose each other and so the package was tied up.

We came from different backgrounds with a variety of skills and disadvantages, but we were all trained social workers. Juliet Horne, the smallest and the youngest, is a psychiatric social worker and had worked in child guidance, special schools and Great Ormond Street Hospital, but not in adoption and never in local authority social services. Hilary Alton had worked only in child care and adoption and only in local authority settings, while I, the oldest of the group, came from a hotch-potch of an early career in the theatre, motherhood, late entry into generic social work and a limited experience of adoption and housing for disabled people. Juliet has a large, close family, Hilary a small dispersed one and I am an only Jewish child with doting parents. None of us is formally religious, none of us adheres to any extreme views, or if we do we have managed to keep them to ourselves. We are all, I suppose, quite strong people because we have made decisions about who we are and what we want, what we have to offer and what we are prepared to do and not to do. Between us we hold and share and use experiences of love and joy, grief and loss, of success and failure, of persecution and acceptance and childlessness and parenthood. By coming to Parents for Children we voted to be uncompetitive and unambitious. There is no career structure and we have put ourselves on one of the sidings of mainstream social work. We also needed and were ready each one of us to put ourselves at risk.

Risk-taking is the essence of our work. There is risk in each unusual placement and that is every one. There is the risk a pioneering agency must take of making wrong assumptions, there is the risk within a small group that there will be an unhealthy inbalance of personalities and that damage will be done to people and there is the ever present risk facing any voluntary agency that its life will come to a sudden end. We have been able to share our risk-taking to a remarkable degree and with remarkable support from our advisers. And the joint decisions which are the result have in turn enabled us to risk ourselves more and to trust one another further.

We do not bear each other's weaknesses gladly but we certainly appreciate each other's positive qualities. Phillida sees all sides of every situation, evaluates each risk and keeps us going in the direction we agree we should take. Juliet is the most volatile, imaginative and theoretical, Hilary the most self-contained, instinctive and creative and I am optimistic and energetic and like to organise. At least that is how we see each other on a good day.

Are we powerful women? It doesn't seem so to us and yet we know exactly what is meant. We are a very small democratic team and we are able to make decisions and execute them more quickly and efficiently than a larger bureaucratic group; each of us knows every aspect of the agency's work because we share it. To be informed and able to make and carry out plans is to seem powerful and in that sense we do have power. To be white and middle class is indefensibly to have power and so in that sense, too, we have power.

Whatever else we are or are seen to be, we are all women. It was not planned that way but that is what happened and goes on happening. None of us had worked in women-only organisations before and we could not know how it would be. It has been and still is good and we do not feel the need to change it, but neither do all of us feel the need to preserve it.

It has been said that we are intimidating and pressurising. An agency with nothing else to do except place children for adoption, however hard they may be to place, must arouse irritation and resentment among social workers with large case loads and hardly enough time to identify children, let alone place them. The referral to us may in itself feel like an admission of failure and then when we place a child for them we also give them more work. Full background information and up-to-date reports on children are necessary if we want to understand their needs, but the energy it takes to collate them may have to be taken away from another case – especially while there are systems like the one that produced five volumes of paper for a thirteen-year-old who has spent her life in care without making a single reference to the 'real child'. The files were full of dutifully completed reviews, 'boarding out' reports, 'change reports', assessment reports, school reports and even psychological reports. These are essential, but where was the record of how she cried when her house-mother left? Where were the descriptions of her original mother and father? Who was holding the memory of the day she got lost, of her first precious toy and all the thousands of things parents would know about their child and adoptive parents will want to know? It is very hard and time consuming for a referring social worker to recapture the life of a child in care.

Finally, after the local authority has done all we have asked, we may come up with an odd kind of family such as they would not have chosen for the child. Our enthusiasm and the way we support each other to justify our decisions must be sickening. But we comfort ourselves that this way the children get placed.

We do not live with our work. Each of us has many interests and relationships which are not part of Parents for Children. Just occasionally, when there is a crisis, it will reach us at home because all our families have our home telephone numbers, but this is never abused. I do remember counting children instead of sheep one night when I could not sleep and had spent the day with a family of fourteen. We do work some evenings and weekends because that is when families are out and about. But on the whole we are also able to plan for our leisure.

Planning is our cornerstone. We make plans together about how to work with every child. We plan the work with every family which responds to a child, we make plans for introductions and placement and for post-placement support and we write it all down and make sure that everyone concerned has a copy. We probably inundate people with our yellow paper. It is surely our need to communicate what we do, to share what we learn and to explain ourselves. It is also our way of defining the risks, of clarifying the issues and of making ourselves accountable. There is a danger in such a small team of doing our own thing. When we began we felt like strangers coming into town and we had to spell everything out. Now there is even more need to be explicit because misconceptions, myths, fantasies and misunderstandings grow with us and we can never be sure we have got it right. When we list our concerns we are threatening and when we keep them to ourselves and get on with it we are withholding and even arrogant. We may be met with resentment, if we insist on making a contribution based on our own gathered experience, but on the other hand the suspicion that we know more than we are telling hovers around. This is not everyone's view of us, but these things have been said; there is always tension and anxiety around placing a child for adoption and on the whole the complaints change to appreciation when a placement works.

We spend a great deal of time talking together informally as we pass each other coming and going or as we happen to be in the office on the same day. More formally with Phillida as she keeps an overall and protective eye on our work load and endlessly as we sit each Wednesday in our team meeting struggling to get through an agenda which includes general agency business and policy, case discussion of individual children and families, publicity, teaching commitments and a constant review of practice through group supervision. We do wonder what our families and other social workers, for whom Wednesday is a day like any other, must make of our Parents for Children Holy Days. Days on which we never visit, go to meetings, teach or make appointments. Only we do of course, it is just another unbreakable rule we occasionally break; but not often. We value the time we can spend together and we need the support we give each other. The appreciation for some piece of work well done, the compassion for a disaster and the caring critical assessment of each other's work. And there is always the time and the framework to make plans with colleagues who share the same beliefs and assumptions and who have the same zany, illogical faith in the impossible. Like Juliet's inspired invention, our green haired Ruritanian monk who lives on the Isle of Wight. We do not, really we do not, make mock of eccentricity, underestimate the traumas of minority groups, the comforts of the Church or the splendours of the Isle of Wight, but in a good humoured way the green haired Ruritanian monk has come to stand for everything that is unlikely, that we do not comprehend, that we cannot predict but that we never discount let alone dismiss.

Now, looking back on nearly seven years together, of close and very arduous work, it seems that shared good humour gets us through. We laugh a great deal and easily. We have developed our own abrasive sense of humour. Juliet has a sharp and glorious wit which can get us going, especially towards the end of long and turgid team meeting days. We can become more and more riotous until faced with tea and five more items on the agenda, Hilary explodes helplessly: 'Decisions, decisions! I can't even choose a bloody biscuit!'

We have surely changed the agency during these seven years and the agency has as surely changed us. We try to remember to ask ourselves: 'Is every change in the best interests of the child?'

6 In the Best Interests of the Child

How can we be sure what is in the best interests of any child? Let alone a child who has been rejected, possibly neglected, who has certainly moved around, changed schools, and been 'in care' of a corporate parent for too long. The corporate or multiple parent begins with the residential social worker or foster parent who knows the child best, but has to refer to the office-based social worker who· holds 'the case', but is accountable to the senior who is supervised by a team leader, and so it goes on until the final responsibility rests with the Director of Social Services who may hardly have heard of the child, but who, like all the parts of this composite parent, will want to serve the child's best interests. And finally, the social services committee made up of elected council members will have to ratify any major decisions the corporate parent makes.

It is hard enough for biological parents who are bringing up their own children to know what is in their best interests. We see how parents agonise on behalf of their children when the time comes to change schools. This school will provide friends in the neighbourhood and is the one the child wants, but it has a discipline problem; that one will offer academic advantages and would stimulate the child's very considerable abilities, and the third is the most progressive and liberal and strong on the arts. There are so many decisions parents must make for their children. Can they be trusted to cross a road, go to stay with a friend, ride a bicycle to school or go youth hostelling on their own? Should they be immunised against whooping cough, have fluoride tablets which will make their teeth strong, but may also make them mottled, or have their tonsils taken out because they get too many colds. Every day some question has to be answered and most parents, knowing their own as well as their child's limitations and capacities, can make good enough decisions with the child's interests at heart, but not all the time. How many parents go to bed at night and wish they had been more firm, or less harsh, had had more time to listen or to think and had done something different because their child has been hurt, upset, misled or has just not understood? Then how can we be certain about children no one really knows?

Biological parents hardly ever have to make the colossal kind of decisions social workers are expected to make. Who can say that James needs a family, if James is as happy as he knows how to be in his hospital school? Was it right to allow him to go through the misery of two failed placements before finding his 'forever' family? Should children living without families and without hope of being able to go back to their birth families be able to choose whether they want to try again? Generally speaking, in our society, we do not ask children to make far-reaching decisions about their lives. If parents have to move, they may or may not take their children's schooling into consideration, but they would not expect a ten-year-old or even a twelve-year-old to decide whether they should move, or when or where to. If parents divorce, they and the judge will make the final decisions about where the children go however much they may take their views into account. Even if fourteen-year-olds have their own ideas they are not independent. At what age should we listen, then, and accept that a child does not want to have new parents or not these new parents? Or should we insist that having a family is in the best interests of every child and that children do not choose their families?

Can we ever begin to know how it must feel to a child like Alice to be given new parents? She has no belief in permanence because she has no experience of it whatsoever and no concepts of family because she has always lived in Children's Homes and she is eight years old. Can we imagine at all how afraid James must have felt going to live in three strange homes and having to pretend he belonged? Not long ago a friend and I went for a working weekend on a farm we did not know and we were put up by a most kindly and easy-going family. But we were not at ease. We were confronted by a system of rules we did not understand. We were not sure when we could have a bath or if we should pull the chain in the night, whether we should help in the house, whether we were expected to sit on our own in the evenings or with the family and the food was not what we were used to. And we were two confident middle aged adults with a home of our own to go back to in two days' time and doing something we had ourselves chosen to do. It was a salutory experience. Not to make us hesitate too long before placing a child, but to make us even more aware of the momentous decisions we must make on behalf of children and that we cannot evade our responsibility or their fear and resistance and pain, although we may in time share some of their joy.

Alice and Bernard came into public care because their young, unmarried mother was turned out by her own parents when she had a second child and she just could not cope on her own although she tried. Alice was only a few weeks old and Bernard not yet two. Their mother wanted them to be adopted and the local authority wanted them to stay together but twelve years ago finding an adoptive family for two black babies was not easy. Alice and Bernard waited while they lived in a residential nursery. They waited until Alice was over a year old and all that time she missed out on mothering while she thrived on excellent care. The parents who were eventually introduced to Bernard and Alice were keen to adopt two children at the same time. They were both doctors in their late thirties, both only children themselves with a biological son just two years older than Bernard. They expected Bernard to be distressed by the move and to be difficult to handle and they expected their own son to be jealous of both newcomers, but they did not expect that Alice would be the most upset and upsetting of the three. She cried inconsolably, but it was impossible to know what for. She did not settle in, fit in, give or even take. She did not know how, while Bernard, who had just enough good experience of early mothering tucked away could begin to respond. It did not ever work for the family and Alice and finally she had to go back to the nursery. This time she lost not only parents, but also her brother. She became ill. She developed asthma. There was something wrong with her hearing. She moved to another Children's Home. She got better. She was still in a Children's Home when she was referred to Parents for Children, but by this time she was nearly eight and a very aggressive, furious and destructive child. Only the housemother could control her, everyone else was scared of her.

Alice scared us too when she came to Parents for Children to prepare for a family. She came once a week and it was three months before she could even look towards a future. By the time the family which was prepared and ready for her, was introduced, she was still not ready to move. There followed six months of stormy weekend and midweek visits, the longest introductions ever known at Parents for Children. But the introductions did not lead anywhere, for nothing would make Alice risk another rejection. So finally (and should we have done it much sooner?) we placed her for adoption screaming and kicking all the way. When she walked into the house she yelled at her courageous new parents, 'And don't think I'm staying for more than twenty years!' A desperate plea for reassurance and security muddled up with a last ditch stand and a pathetic ignorance about families.

Alice went on screaming and kicking for a long time; years after adoption she is still screaming and kicking and it is a struggle for the family to keep going. Was it justified to make Alice move, was it fair to her or to her adoptive family? Should we have listened harder, waited longer, prepared her more, or were we right to say that the parents were the best people to make it work for her? Should we have found another family, avoided conflict and the idea of a 'make or break' situation? Or was it enough that Alice wrote a story at school about a starfish who did not have a family and never got a family, for at the end of that story Alice wrote, 'Poor starfish'.

Sandra was perhaps even more hostile than Alice to the idea of a new family. She was fostered until two years ago. She always felt an outsider in the foster family and punished her foster parents until they gave up. When she came to us she was punishing herself. She really hated herself and was sure that no one would ever want her if they knew her. She liked coming to our office and worked hard on making the book

with her life story, but threw her food about like a toddler.
While she was getting to know herself she was expelled from
school and was in trouble with the police. She had a vocabu-
lary almost entirely made up of swear words, but she spoke so
indistinctly that not too many were offended. She had become
a runner and ran from anything and anyone she did not like
and there was very little that she did like. She ran away from the
first parents we found for her. An elaborate plan to move
Sandra to a unique family fully prepared to accept her and
hold her still resulted in a fight in the car on the way. In the
middle of oral abuse and attempts to scratch and punch and
bite, Sandra yelled: 'You're doing this on purpose!' It seemed
so absurd that anyone could casually or accidentally escort a
tragic, screeching adolescent across London that for a
moment we both laughed. But it was a moment of truth. We
were doing it on purpose and she was beginning to show signs
that she wanted adults with a purpose to take control. When
we had arrived at her new home and she had spat and sulked,
we made a contract which we signed, with her new mother,
her local authority social worker and Parents for Children. We
solemnly declared that whensoever Sandra ran and whereso-
ever she ran to, she would be brought back to this family.
Sandra never ran again. Two years after placement she is
ready to be adopted and she will be.

The final judgement about Sandra's placement was made
by Doris, another teenager. Doris, nearly sixteen, more confident, ambitious, and with a good idea of the alternatives,
understood that adoption, unlike everything else, was for life
– 'not just for when you're a kid.' She had been fostered, lived
in a Children's Home and now she wanted a family of her own.
But her fantasy of a family could never match the reality and
after trying three times by getting to know three families,
Doris decided, with our help, that she was better off where she
was. She said she would like to keep the last family she met as
friends, but she was really looking forward to moving to a
hostel with her mates and later into a flat. When she came to
Parents for Children to say goodbye she looked at Sandra's
picture and said, 'She's lucky.' I couldn't think what Doris
meant, so I asked her. 'Well', she said, 'she's young enough to
be made to go.'

What is young enough? Children with special needs do not necessarily function according to their chronological age. Most disconcertingly they can appear to be old for their years in one way and young in another at one and the same time, because their development has been inconsistently affected and delayed by all the stops and starts in their lives. So a girl who already looks like a woman may make the emotional demands and responses of a toddler; she may competently put a younger brother to bed, but be too scared to sleep with the door closed. She may be clever at school but her parents may observe that 'she hasn't got the sense she was born with.' It is hard to know what is in the best interests of a boy who wants to sit on every adult's lap and has the power and the inclination to get his own way by using force.

Ernie was fourteen, physically mature, mentally more like a ten-year-old, and far more attached than anyone realised to the housemother and Children's Home he had known all his life. He thought he wanted a family, he pleaded for a second chance after he refused the first family he was introduced to, he moved in with the next family with only a slight push, but he could not find the incentive to make it work. Ernie liked the attention he got when plans were made for him and he enthusiastically joined in the game of finding parents although deep down, possibly even without knowing it, he never for a moment contemplated using a family for more than the treats and presents he could get out of them. He said, 'If you make me stay I'll win the battle.' And he did. He saw everything in terms of winning and losing and he used violence to win; he was as tall as his single mother and stronger and he used his strength to tyrannise.

Sadly we felt it was too late for Ernie because he was too big to be physically held by a family against his will and he was emotionally too retarded to make an investment in family life. We had to accept that he should not be placed again.

It seemed in Ernie's best interests to return to his Children's Home and to the housemother who was the only really significant person in his life. If she stays long enough she will be able to see him through his career in care and help him to move away when he is eighteen. Unless this Children's Home, like so many others, has to close down before then. We failed

Ernie because it had taken nearly two years to find those two families for him and in those two years he had changed from a young boy to a young man.

Danny, on the other hand, was already fourteen when he was referred to us and quite grown up. He was a withdrawn boy who made few demands but he was determined to have a family for the future. He had no experience of family life whatever, but neither did he have Doris' unrealistic expectation and prejudice. Small wonder that not many of them adopt a child with special needs who could make an irrational claim on scarce time and resources.

We hoped it was in his best interests to be adopted.

7   Black Children

We have not been successful in placing black children with black families. We have always aimed to find black parents for black children but we have failed. Our optimism leads us to believe that we have not tried hard enough in the right way, in the right places at the right time, because we know other agencies have succeeded. When black families have come forward in response to Parents for Children's publicity they have withdrawn again quite quickly. In America it also took time and an increase of racial awareness on everyone's part before nearly all black children could be placed with black families. A large part of the British black community is still made up of first and second generation immigrants rebuilding their own families often against a background of discrimination and prejudice. Small wonder that not many of them adopt a child with special needs who could make an irrational claim on scarce time and resources.

We are very aware that we are all white adoption workers and that a black worker might have done better; we know a black worker would have helped the black children who have joined white families in a way we probably cannot. Black workers have not applied for the jobs; again, the need may not have been communicated where it could be heard, but it may also be that the very specialised work we do is not a priority for politically conscious black workers who are in demand in the community.

So we have placed black children with white families hoping that they will have a better experience of living in a multi-racial society than they have had so far. Without exception, the black children referred to us had grown up in predominantly white Children's Homes or with white foster families.

They probably did not even meet any black children living with their own black families because all the other black children they knew were also in care. Almost all saw themselves as white children with black skins and some of the mentally handicapped black children were described as unaware of race. When we worked with the children to prepare them for family life, most of them asked for white parents because everything in their lives led them to think that white does best. On television, in school, in comics, the view that white is more often right is carelessly upheld. Heroes in books are usually white while the villain if not literally black is still a black villain. An intelligent girl like Doris sums up that a white aspiring family may get her further than an equally bright black one. After all, the successful people she has come into contact with during sixteen years in care are white. The black people she knows do the cooking and the washing and go on the buses. She does not want to do that when she grows up.

Ernie's only memory of a black family is his mother who injured him when he was very small and he is angry with all black people. He says he does not ever want anyone to know he is black. He has been bewildered by the newsreels of anti-police riots. He does not want to be part of all that confrontation; he is already scared of the violence inside him which he cannot handle. Well meaning carers comfort him, tell him that he is safe and far away from the troubles. We found a single parent for Ernie, a white woman who lived among black friends in a multiracial area. She got him into a special school for slow learners where some of the teachers and many of the children were black. She introduced him to black families who were friendly and to black men who were the kind of people Ernie admired. They bought their groceries from black shopkeepers and went to a black hairdresser so that Ernie began to take a pride in his appearance. This was one of the placements that did not last and Ernie is back in his Children's Home where he wants to remain. But although it is a long way from where he lives, Ernie has chosen to stay in the school with other black children and all on his own, once a month, he goes to the black hairdresser. He also visits his single parent that wasn't and her black friends. Not a success story certainly but perhaps Ernie learned and accepted that he was not so far from those riots after all.

We cannot guarantee that all the white families who adopt black children will do as well as Ernie's single parent tried to do in the short time he was with her. Some adoptive parents have a way of not doing exactly what they meant to do when the child becomes their own. So, to our embarrassment, some families tell us that their black child has no feelings about being different, never talks about it, never asks anything, does not seem to notice, has no black friends, does not meet other black people, and is after all just like the rest of us. Other families struggle to provide black contacts and to make their children racially conscious and confident, but the struggle is uphill because our society is not nearly as multiracial as we should like to think for our comfort.

Some families learn on the job. The Deightons adopted Jenny when she was ten. She had been abused as a small child and then suffered from an unidentified illness. She was mentally retarded, slightly lame and completely confused. She could see very little and spoke timidly with fear in her eyes and an occasional secret smile. She was and still is a radiant child, with a tremulous quality, a silent invitation to take care of her, a mute accusation about what has happened to her. It hurt to work with Jenny and her new parents have been hurt many times. And Jenny, even while becoming their daughter, has got worse not better. She has developed a very severe kind of epilepsy, her eyesight has deteriorated further and her future is uncertain, but she may end up in a wheelchair, and she will certainly remain dependent on her family.

Jenny is African British and the Deightons had looked after many African children while their parents studied, but race was not uppermost in their minds as they tried to deal with the many acute problems Jenny brought with her. As time went by and Jenny became more content but also more handicapped, it seemed unnecessary to bother her with ideas she did not appear to have. Sometimes she was teased because she was spastic and surely that was enough? There were no other black children in the village, Jenny's parents felt quite at ease with their black daughter and reluctantly we agreed that Jenny was really a child who would not understand and that having a family was more important. In due course James joined this same family, and he was certainly pleased to find a black sister, but his new sister seemed not to notice the likeness. When she was fourteen Jenny had to go to a special boarding school because her epilepsy was uncontrollable and she became a danger to herself. It is a happy school and Jenny had had four good years of family life to help her make the most of it. She met her first boyfriend there and telephoned home bubbling with excitement, but all she could say was, 'He's brown, just like me, you know, he's lovely and brown.' Her parents were amazed, but they were also pleased that they had given her the message that black, or brown, as Jenny observed, is lovely. They will not think again that Jenny or any other child, however disabled, limited or retarded, does not need to know. And as they learned we learned with them.

Every time we place a black child with a white family we ask them and ourselves the same questions. Do they want a black child because they want that child or because that child is black? Because they see themselves and their children as members of a multiracial society or because they need to prove a point? Because they think it does not matter either way and there is no difference, because they like being parents and a child with special needs needs them or because they move easily and respectfully among all people and will teach their children ease and respect? Do white parents have black friends their children will be able to identify with and value – or how will they grown up to value themselves in a country where nearly all important people are white? Are they the kind of parents who would join 'Harmony', a mutually supportive group of multiracial, multicultural families? Will they be able to deal lovingly with black hair and skin? Will they make their child more aware and proud of roots, culture and race? Will they be able to help their black daughter or son to withstand name-calling, bullying, being picked on or passed over, the daily translations of prejudice and discrimination? And finally will they be able, if the need arises, to help their child to stand up and be counted?

There are some wrong answers and we would not want to place black children with people who tell us that they really want a white child, but would be prepared to take on a mixed-race child, not too dark; nor with people who say that being black is as good as being white and they are not prejudiced. There are no quite right answers, however, and all we can do is to explore attitudes and feelings together with the white families who come forward for black children. Children who have already been left behind and cannot afford to wait much longer.

Tony has now lost all his milk teeth and has had one silver coin for each of them. He and his younger brother Norman and younger sister Belinda have been adopted by a childless white couple and they live and thrive on their farm. The children are British West Indian. One room in the farmhouse is filled with photographs of the West Indies, pictures of Asian and African men and women are cut out of magazines and pinned up and the lives and careers of well known black personalities are followed avidly by the whole family. When I visit and clearly don't know who the black pop star is or the black sportsman, I am chided with tolerant amusement for my ignorance, but if I do a little better with black politicians I rise in the children's estimation.

On the farm there are animals and the children watch them breed and are particularly fond of the black and white lambs which are born when the black sheep are mated with the white sheep. When Belinda's class was invited to visit the farm, the highlight of the school outing was seeing how the large dairy herd was milked and fed with the help of a computer which makes space invaders boring by comparison. During the demonstration two children were asked to volunteer to be cows. They were understandably shy so Belinda took charge. 'I'll be the black cow', she said and turning to a pale little boy addressed him authoritively, 'and you be the white.'

A year ago these parents wanted a fourth child. They did not consider a white one and were not too keen on a light one. They did not want the new child to feel left out and they did not want one adopted child to look more like the parents than the other three. These seemed sensible reasons and we supported them because as far as we could tell they were in the best interests of the children they already had and the child they wanted to have. But they admitted that there was another reason: 'White children look as though they weren't finished.'

However idyllic, a remote farm with white parents cannot be perfect for black children; but it is good enough surely and good enough parenting is what we look for when we seek adoptive families. And when we try to measure what is good enough, we have to measure it not against what we would like to be able to offer but against what is available. The choice has not been between a white family and a black family but between a white family and a white Children's Home.

We will never get it exactly right for any child. Phillida, Hilary, Juliet and I can never really know how it feels to be black or to be adopted. Or indeed how it feels to be disabled, to be in care or to grow up without families. We cannot even know how it feels to be a man, to be a coalminer or to be a priest. Half the people we work with are men. If we had to experience everything for ourselves in order to be effective we would become immobilised. We do have some relevant living behind us and a skilful adoption panel to guide us and we can only make the most of that. Yes we would be a more balanced team if at least one of us was black and one a man and if we were not all middle class. And yes all black children should have black parents and like any child they would prefer it if the need to be adopted did not arise in the first place.

8 Using Publicity

'What about the *Farmer's Weekly*?' is the recurring cry when nothing else has brought in the enquiring families and a child is waiting. We also have our fantasies, and one of our favourites is the one about the damaged, disabled city child who will find acceptance and love and plenty among the lambs and the green fields. We have placed children with two farming families and our fantasies came true, but unfortunately neither of them heard about their children through the *Farmer's Weekly*. To be fair one of them saw the letter we had written to the *Farmer's Weekly* mentioned in their local paper and took it from there, but the article in that paper would have got their attention anyway. We still feel that we should do more to reach people in country areas who may never have thought of adopting an older or handicapped child; and we are convinced that every kind of publicity has to be used to make the great public aware of the possibility and the need.

Is all publicity good publicity? Yes, if it increases this awareness and gets even one child placed with one family. And that may not be immediately because the best publicity has a habit of causing a small stir and making a few ripples that go on and on and may be picked up even years later in a dentist's waiting room or may lodge in someone's mind and reappear when the moment is right.

Putting an advertisement in a newspaper is one thing, persuading a journalist to write a feature article about a child is quite another. An advertisement can be disguised or anonymous; it is often unjustly accused of selling children like puppies, it is short lived and it is expensive. A feature in a newspaper or magazine has the value of being a true story, of being written in a style that readers like, of being illustrated and free. Some magazines have invited us to write our own articles and have even paid us for them, but just arousing the interest of one journalist is more work than placing an advertisement. Co-ordinating the children and the families to meet a reporter, to be excused from school or to take time off from work and getting permission for the children to be featured can be a daunting task. We analysed the effort made to organise one major piece of publicity in a national newspaper.

There was a whole morning in the office for two workers while the children were interviewed; thirty-four telephone calls had to be made and ten letters were written to make the necessary arrangements. Initially five hours had been spent making contact with the reporter, filling in the background for her, explaining our attitudes and discussing which children should be featured. Then the three chosen children and their houseparents had to be thoroughly briefed by their Parents for Children workers for the interview and after the article appeared they had to be kept informed about the responses and given the time to talk about the feelings aroused by the publicity. We had to put time aside to deal with one hundred and twenty calls and letters. We had to prepare an information pack to send out to enquirers by return of post, and we invited those still interested to an evening open meeting within two weeks of the article appearing. At the open meeting we spoke to them about the children in the newspaper and about other children who needed families. They saw photographs and slides and met some of the Parents for Children staff and some adoptive parents. They heard about the way we work and could make up their own minds whether they wanted to pursue one of the children and whether they wanted to work with us. Two children were adopted as a direct result and that is a bigger return that we ever expected. One child placed would have justified the undertaking – even none would have made us want to do it again given the chance. And when we get the chance for television and radio publicity we use it gladly although it entails even more work.

There was a time when we felt dubious and anxious about the popular press. We feared that the children would be exploited, the natural parents attacked and the agency misunderstood. This has certainly not happened; it was we who misunderstood and we have had to learn about journalists and the media so that we can try to match our expectation to what is on offer rather than stick to preconceived ideas of what is good publicity and what is not. We have had to accept that we often cannot say what must go in or stay out of an article, but we realise that journalists want to get it right too. We may still quibble about reports that miss a vital point and we may still flinch at a headline superimposed by a sub-editor but Mickey would not have found his family without it. 'Kids in Search of Love' it said, in the boldest print and underneath it 'Still Smiling – Three Homeless Orphans.'

Mickey was not an orphan and he was not homeless, but he was one of the children we thought we might not place. His story was one of the saddest, he was one of the most dejected children we have met and he was fourteen years old. Even when he was in care everyone seemed to prefer one of his many brothers and sisters. When he came to Parents for Children he would not make a poster, but he allowed Phillida to make one for him. On a large yellow sheet of paper she stuck his photograph and wrote underneath: 'Mickey doesn't want to make a poster but he does want a family'. Only we did not understand just how much and we have marvelled time and time again at the depth of a child's desire to belong.

We wanted to avoid anything like formal introductions for Mickey because he behaved aggressively at the slightest provocation and was likely to refuse designated parents on sight. So the family which had seen him in the newspaper came to tea in the Children's Home, casually, as friends of the staff sometimes do. And Mickey claimed them for himself without hesitation though for a time he was too afraid to acknowledge them as real substitutes for his dream parents. Then one day he rang them from the Children's Home and they heard him say to the other boys who were being noisy: 'Shut up, I'm speaking to my old man.' If ever there was a right family for a child it was this family for this child. There have been plenty of difficulties but none these parents could not handle and Mickey is now adopted. It is one of our nightmares rather than fantasies that we might not have found Mickey's parents for we would not have found them without that headline that worried us so.

Apart from Mickey, all the children who were old enough have made, or at least have helped to make, their own posters about themselves. They like seeing their work up on the wall and they can see immediately that they are not the only ones – other children need families too. And they learn that families will see their posters because families also come to Parents for Children to work.

The children can make any kind of poster as long as it is brown and yellow. At least that is how it began, but recently other colours have been creeping in requested by the children and encouraged by the workers who are feeling that what once provided unity now threatens constraint. Some children want to create works of art, others want to fill the space with every available snapshot, drawing, and all the information about themselves they can muster. Edward used two sheets of paper to make the biggest ever; he was six feet four inches tall and fifteen years old and it was most important to him to make the two sheets look all of a piece. Sandra added something to her poster every time she came to the office. She was as dissatisfied with it as she was with herself. Disabled children can become very involved in making their posters and be quite sure of what they want people to know about them; Harry insisted that any future Dad must know that he is an Arsenal supporter. Ernie finished his poster and put it up and stood back and asked: 'Do you think when people see it they will say "that's a nice little boy"?'

Posters get moved from one side of the room to the other when children are introduced to their families and when they join the family the posters are taken down and a photograph of the child and the new family is put up in a special place. The children who come to work with us can see the progress other children make towards adoption and they can see that some move quickly and some take a long time. They can see that there are many different kinds of families and they can see that it does not always work the first time because just sometimes children move back to the wall they came from. James, when asked by a sympathetic new teacher about what happens when you get adopted, explained: 'You move your poster to the other wall.'

Whenever possible children also help to write descriptions

of themselves for their own photosheets which get sent out to an ever lengthening mailing list of adopters and would-be adopters. Everyone who contacts us and all the families who work with us are put on the mailing list unless they choose not to be. The children understand that their photosheets are sent to hundreds of people; they help to duplicate them and to stuff the envelopes if they can or they watch if they cannot. In this way they begin to realise that new parents will be interested in them, want to know about them and will be able to accept them 'warts and all'. It is usually a great relief to children to know that they do not have to pretend to be good and most of them like making a list of their 'warts'. They may even ask us to make sure that parents-to-be know all the bad things about them before they are introduced. This will not ensure better behaviour when the time comes – there are no insurance policies in adoption – but it may make the worst happen sooner.

Children enjoy publicity. They respond to the attention and are usually relieved to know that something is happening, that someone is really looking for a family, that they are important enough to bother about. Very few children mind about making their need for a family known. It is shameful that they are without families – not that they say so publicly and children have taught us that any embarrassment we feel about publicity is our problem not theirs. We may feel guilty about what has been allowed to happen to a child, but must not feel so guilty that we hush it up. When children do object to publicity it is nearly always because they have been made to feel that they are to blame for their fate, or because they want to protect their original parents from the hurt of seeing it all written down. They should never be allowed to fear that they will not get parents if they do not want publicity. Each child has to understand that while publicity may find families for some children it will not necessarily work for them, not this time anyway; on the other hand they may find parents through other children's efforts. Doris particularly liked this idea. She is an articulate girl with strong views and she made publicity a way of life. She was interviewed, recorded, photographed and televised and used the media to work out her own feelings and ideas. Even after she decided she was not for a family, she went on recruiting for other children.

If children are not to be made to feel ashamed of who they are, we should not disguise them by giving them false names or hide them by not using photographs. We have always used the children's own first names for all publicity and would not be prepared to do otherwise. Children in care can be confused enough about their identity and we must not confuse them further. Changing names does not get more parents, but will lose some on the way. Not only do children feel confused if they are disguised, but families feel resentful if Johnny is not Johnny and it starts them off on the wrong foot. There is a place, to be sure, for protecting privacy and this book will not betray who is who, but this book is not seeking parents for James, who is not really James, because he already has them.

Whether we use newspapers, magazines, radio, television or just our own photosheets and mailing list, all the families who have adopted through Parents for Children first saw their particular child in some form of publicity. We never suggest a child to a family, we always wait for the family's reaction to a child. And by now we know that families always know best. We have also discovered that a beautiful child will not necessarily draw a bigger response than a plain one, so we have stopped minding about misleading lovely photographs though of course we would always want photographs to look like the child and preferably like the full length one. At the beginning of 1983 we had three handicapped babies to place. One seemed to us far less attractive than the other two, but several families enquired about him because they each thought that no one else would. The appeal it seems is not in looks but in need. If the media cannot be persuaded to publicise that need, we can all use the media by writing letters to magazines and newspapers, phoning in on radio programmes, sending out press releases and getting in on chat shows. There is no end to the means by which we can communicate.

We have tried and are still trying to explore various ways of using leaflets and posters for more general publicity purposes but it has been difficult to gauge results. Posters in doctors' surgeries and Health Centres may have raised the level of consciousness about adoption of hard-to-place children, but we do not really know if that is so. Leafleting the congregation of an evangelical church did not bring the hoped for black adopters, but it might have done and may still do. Our latest experiment is a poster in the outer stations of the London Underground with an idea borrowed from Bertie Bassett and kindly financed by George Bassett and Co. It was thought up in a moment of hilarity, brought on by desperation, at a time when we felt we were not making contact with enough new people. The sketch we made that day showed Liquorice All Sorts of people and children and the wording said 'All Sorts of Children need All Sorts of Parents'. In our excitement we didn't doubt that we could interest Bassetts in our brainchild and that they would not only give us permission to use their trade mark but might also pay for the campaign. And that is exactly how it turned out. We were lucky enough to have a public relations man working with us during the four months it took to get from idea to bill posting so that we were able to enjoy the progress without having to do the spade work; but the wonder of it was to be working in an environment where ideas could be taken up and developed and with some energy put into practice.

We never underestimate the importance of speaking. We speak to people whenever we can and try never to refuse an invitation. People who listen in a church hall in Basingstoke may have a friend who will finally adopt or there may be an elderly woman among them who didn't realise that children also need grandmothers. Foster parents may become adopters if they hear the necessary information and parents who have adopted already may find room for a child with special needs. Clubs, institutes and trade associations provide rich hunting grounds and some of them will follow up with articles in specialist journals. We each spend roughly one and a half days a month speaking and much of that is teaching and training. We are involved in workshops for social workers and we talk to students in schools of social work. Part of our brief is to publicise what we do, to enable others to do it and finally to talk ourselves out of a job.

Perhaps our most spectacular publicity to date was our appeal on BBC Television in January 1980. We asked Brian Murphy, the actor of 'George and Mildred' fame, to speak for us because we knew of his interest in adoption, and he did us proud. People wrote in and sent money ranging from less than fifty pence to more than a hundred pounds. We were humbled by the widows' mites, the people's generosity and the children's contributions. But we were overwhelmed by the interest, the well-wishers and the understanding of children's needs. And we were intensely proud, because Brian Murphy was speaking of our families and the five minute film showed two of those families and we heard them tell Brian Murphy what it was all about. There is no better publicity for adoption than for parents and children who have done it to talk to the rest of us. Of course there are always exceptions. An adoptive father who was interviewed by the press tried to explain about the care adoption agencies must take, however informally they work. He told the startled reporter that Parents for Children 'finds out all about your record for assaulting children' and she printed that.

9 Funny Children Need Funny Families

The children we place are not ordinary children and we would not want to find them ordinary families, even if there were such families about. The children we place are special because they have special needs and the families who adopt them are special because they have special needs too. 'Special' in the sense of being unusual, not better than good, and the need is to give as well as to take from each other.

Josephine is five. She is blind, she has diabetes insipidus, a serious growth hormone deficiency, and we do not know yet how mentally retarded she will be. A very special child indeed. Her adoptive parents are nurses and skilled in massage and other touch techniques. They have both been married before and have brought up seven children between them. They are Jehovah's Witnesses. They are deeply religious and they do not accept blood transfusions. They are no longer very young. Are they a funny family for a funny child? We certainly had to widen our horizons to take on Josephine for many people said this child was not adoptable.

It is always a question of widening the horizons and never of lowering the sights. When older and handicapped children were first considered for adoption, critics said unkindly that we were finding second class families for second class children. Never. The opposite is true. The challenging child needs parents with something extra to offer.

When Josephine went to court to be adopted, the Judge said some flattering things to the mother and father who had accepted a task without an end which included monitoring Josephine's fluid level at hourly intervals throughout the night. When he had finished they explained; 'We are all dependent but she's a little girl who gives.'

People with something extra to give are not necessarily appreciated. Families who work with Parents for Children have more often than not been turned down as adopters by other agencies, because they are unconventional, do not fit the criteria, and may even seem eccentric. Single parents, older couples, families with many children already and people who have been divorced have traditionally not been accepted. But single parents can be the right parents, older children do not need very young couples, large families have invaluable experience and divorced people may have learnt something useful from their mistakes.

Some adults do not like babies, some people want a child who will remain dependent and some can never have enough children. But these reasons for wanting to adopt older children, handicapped children or just more children have been said to be questionable. Life styles have been criticised as unsatisfactory, but what looks like a jumble to one family, can seem like riches to another and both could be comfortable with their own way of life and share that comfort with a child. Adoption workers do not have to live with either.

Prospective adopters in less than perfect health have been turned down many times and one young wife and husband who came to Parents for Children had made a file of the thirty-three rejections they received in answer to their country-wide enquiries. The wife was a health visitor who spent her working life advising mothers and handling babies, but she was also an epileptic. They have made wonderful adoptive parents to a physically disabled toddler and now have a baby of their own.

Space is another of the great issues. Who can tell whether a family has room for one more? The Deightons like to think of themselves as just an ordinary family. When they first came to Parents for Children because they wanted Jenny, their three home grown children still lived with them, they already had a handicapped baby they planned to adopt and they lived in a three bedroomed terraced house. They were not over-crowded because they did not feel overcrowded. It did not really matter how they arranged themselves around their home; it was never a problem. They moved after three years to a larger house on another estate. And they filled it up quickly, with James and then with Brendan, a teenager in need of protection and guidance and (is it finally?) with Nina, a Down's syndrome baby. This ordinary family does what experts, professionals and biological parents have failed to do. There may be something eccentric about families who can always find room for one more but an overriding love and compassion for children is not a disadvantage for would-be adopters.

'We can give lots of love and cooking,' wrote one of our first families, and there is no better way of saying it. We are lucky when we find 'love and cooking' families. Then there are the families who 'weave their own oatcakes', Juliet's fond description of parents who make and grow and build and knit and include children in their creativity. Their homes may be a curious clutter and their budgeting a muddle and their routine chaotic, but some children do best in the middle of such outward confusion. Others need to have an order imposed upon them; they may need parents with strong views, firm methods and a strict moral code; or a single parent who does not have to divide her attention or a couple who can focus on one precious child. There are no good, better, best families. There are only families which are right for each child because their needs and the child's needs somehow fit, and what they have to offer each other is more or less what they are both looking for. We recognise, though, that some families can stretch to make the fit more comfortable and that some circumstances can help them to stretch.

We know that fathers on shifts, taxi drivers, railway workers, miners, farmers, industrial workers, policemen and ministers of the Church are able to spend more time with their children than regular workers and adopted children need time. We know that a significant proportion of our families are deeply religious and that their driving force and support and guidance comes from their religion. We know that many parents have chosen to adopt children who need them, because being parents is what they enjoy being most and they know they are good at it.

Social workers and teachers are said not to make good adopters and if they are like us, we begin to see all the logical reasons why it should not work because we ourselves could not do it. Yet we have teachers and social workers among our families and we are grateful to them for proving to us again and again that there are no right ingredients for right families.

We do not seek ideal parents because we feel it is more important for a child to have 'good enough' parents quickly which is surely what most children have. We hope that all the families who adopt will be able to express tenderness because that is what all children need. We try not to have preconceived ideas about the kind of family we are looking for. We do not attempt to replace the child's family of origin with a similar kind of family, nor necessarily with a different kind.

Dawn was wary of male children. She had been displaced by two younger brothers in her natural family so we did not look for an adoptive family with boys. When the Newsomes came along they had one son younger than Dawn, but in spite of our fears, she related well and affectionately to her new brother. Trouble came when the parents decided to adopt again and they chose another, younger boy, thus making themselves into a replica of Dawn's original family. Now Dawn, aged fourteen, became frenzied in her need to find out if she would be displaced again. She stayed out at night, was expelled from two schools and brought her parents to the point where they wondered whether they could really carry on with this virago in the home. When rows in the family seemed to be all there was, Dawn went to stay with friends and stayed away for seven weeks, only visiting her adoptive parents occasionally, to have a polite cup of tea with them, as strangers do.

In the end Gerald and Iris Newsome decided that it was time for Dawn to come home and they brought her back to the house and told her that however hard it was for them to be together, together they belonged and together they would stay. Dawn learned that it was safe to go away and to come back. She could finally believe that boys did not necessarily get a better deal than girls and that the two adoptive brothers whom she loved would not cause her to be sent away. Dawn's outrageous behaviour stopped. She had been offered a place in another school. She works conscientiously at a part time job in a riding stable and she is allowing herself to grow up.

We respect that parents have a very clear idea about the kind of children they want and we would not try to change their minds. What we predict as being right for a family is often proved wrong when they show interest in a very different child. We thought one childless couple would start with a younger girl but they fell for a teenager who reminded them of an uncle and although all Nick wanted to say about himself on his poster was that he had adopted a swan, it was the very thing the new parents wanted to hear.

But sometimes people change their minds because there is a child who needs them. Danny's parents had two little boys already and were only in their middle twenties. They came to Parents for Children because they thought they could adopt a handicapped baby girl. Then they saw Danny's poster, they heard his story and they were hooked on a fourteen-year-old boy. They were not even old enough to have been his parents and they had never thought of building a family by adding an eldest son, but they became his parents nevertheless and Danny was glad to have such a young family.

Not all parents find it easy to make that first visit to Parents for Children. Helen and Mathew married quite late in life. They were unable to have a child and were considered too old to adopt by the agencies they approached. Then they heard of Parents for Children and after much heart searching decided that they could love a handicapped child just as well as an ordinary one. They made an appointment and travelled up to London by train. 'We got as far as Paddington Station,' said Helen 'and then we both had a terrible panic and felt we couldn't go on with it so we phoned Parents for Children and apologised and said we just weren't interested any more and went back home.' A few weeks later they received our photo-sheet of Rachel, a blonde, solemn Down's syndrome child, and they made another appointment and in due course Rachel became their daughter.

We do not recruit families and then select them out. We select them in. We believe that if we begin by asking questions, by putting up hurdles, by delving into private lives, we end up by making adoption an endurance test or an obstacle race and tests and races are there to be completed and won. We do not want people to go on and on in order to complete the course or to feel they have to win a child. Parents could surely deceive us and confuse us, if they had a mind to, and we do not want to give them cause.

We aim to relate all our work with families to the needs of one particular child and to explore with them how far they can meet those needs and their own by adopting that child. We are looking at the parents and the parents are looking at us as representatives of the child and the agency. In due course they see the child's file. It is a two-way appraisal and a self-appraisal. Could these parents enjoy this child now or would they always be waiting for an improvement which might never come? How does their family function and can it go on functioning in the same way with the new child? Where would adjustments have to be made? How do they get their rewards and what are their supports and do they have enough? Do husbands and wives regard each other as good mothers and fathers? How might the family's children, grandparents and neighbours react to this adoption? We do not try to make it hard for parents, but we want them to have a realistic grasp of what they are wanting to do.

No one wants to have a child who will not be able to fit into their family or would damage their other children or would be damaged by them. It is as important to help some families to withdraw as it is to enable others to carry on. People who come to an adoption agency have a right to a service which not only pursues the best interests of the child, but also does not lead adults into damaging experiences. Yet, finally, if we work honestly and openly with adults we cannot protect them from the risks they are willing to take. And so perhaps the essence of preparing adopters is to identify the risks, to share them and neither to exaggerate them nor to underestimate them. The risks are never the same, each placement carries its very own risk factor, but the risks are getting bigger. As the children become more and more hard to place, so the risks involved become harder to take.

Josephine's parents say that they are now ready to have Sheeraz who is two years old and weighs only fifteen pounds; she is deaf, blind and mentally retarded; we know they are a skilled family, they say they can do it, the alternatives for Sheeraz are bleak. Should we do more than point out the considerable risks? Can they possibly have the energy to bring up two such seriously handicapped children? The mother has brought up five, single handed, and nursed one with leukaemia until she died. Can they give both children the attention they need? They are surrounded by supportive family and friends. What if Sheeraz should need a blood transfusion which for them would be a violation of God's law? Do we not have to weigh the possible death of a truly loved child, who this family believe would be brought back to life in God's good time, against a probable lifetime in institutions or in a series of foster homes? Sheeraz could wait for another family to adopt her which may never turn up and if it does, might not have that very quality which enables Josephine's parents to do the impossible but also makes them accept a prohibition on blood transfusions. They say that their strength comes from God, through religion. If we think they are good parents, we cannot then quibble about what God says or means, any more than we can quibble with other parents about the way they handle their children. If we accept that they are the right parents for a child we have also to accept their ways, however strange they may seem to us. We cannot expect parents to take risks without shouldering some ourselves. And we must not expect parents, who are doing something we could not do, to bring up their children in the way we would.

We ask people to come and see the way we work and to decide whether they want to work with us. We hold open meetings for all comers once a month. Olive is an old age pensioner, a widow, and children have been her life. She came to an open meeting and heard us say that people who love children so much that they cannot live without them often make very good parents. After the meeting she stayed behind and had a good, long chat. She had always been made to feel that she was too old and a bit peculiar to keep on and on about children. Could she have another? She went on to have a teenager with a fatal disease.

We hold a series of adoption classes. We aim to enable the group to exchange experiences of children and childhood and parents and families. We have devised a series of activities and exercises to explore the stages of human growth and development and the remembrance of separation and loss.

We link adopters-to-be with parents who have done it and we encourage them to find out about their own local schools, parents' groups and provision for handicapped children.

Afterwards adopters have remembered what went on in groups, but have been more vague about the content of our home visits and even uncertain about the purpose of them except, as they say, that it was a good way of getting to know and trust each other. We are now putting more and more emphasis on shared doing and less and less value on the ground we cover by talking about it. Family trees, diaries, recording a day of family life, diagrams of how the family sees its place in the community and lists of family rules and rituals as well as games with the family's children, can produce more helpful material for parents than any amount of abstract discussion about upbringing, discipline, motivation, infertility and sex. Not that any of that is unimportant, if it is relevant to the child they have in mind, but it will be more relevant if the parents can make their own connections.

Some people like to write and will do better at writing reports about themselves than we would, some will devour every adoption book in print and some will not even bother to read the simplest leaflet. Some families are not used to dealing with words, but are well used to dealing with children. Some will join every parents' group and pressure group available, others will sniff the air and decide to do their own thing, while others still will not venture forth.

Whichever way families work we try to follow their lead and to go at their pace and we always try to be clear about the next step. Some families can race ahead and some need to go slowly. Some do most of the work on their own between visits and some rely on us to see them through each stage. Whichever way we work together and however careful the preparation, the first thing that causes a problem will, as likely as not, be something none of us had thought would be important. We were caught up with Margery's disabilities; she was fourteen, in a wheelchair and utterly dependent for all her needs and bodily functions. We made sure that her handicaps were understood but we overlooked her tiresome habit of telling fibs about all things at all times. Her single mother managed everything else but it was the fibbing that nearly broke up the placement.

There must clearly be times when we, the workers, do not agree with the people who want to adopt. We are accountable for the placements we make and however far we move towards working together, we have to take responsibility for recommending to an adoption panel who should adopt whom. There have been few occasions in seven years when we have not taken families along with us all the way but there have been some.

There was the sad couple with a history of violence whose application we could not, in all conscience, support for any of the children we would have to place; and there was a severely disabled mother who had one child already and we would not place another. They were angry about our decision and we cannot be sure that we were right not to be moved. For we do want parents who will fight to have their children. Like the Newsomes, when we told them on the telephone that we felt they already had enough on their plate with sorting out their own fraught and complex family situation. They got in the car and drove fifty miles to see us immediately and we agreed there and then to proceed. They are the couple who adopted Dawn, one of the most challenging girls we have placed.

Some families have agreed that we shall never have the right child for them and have tried to find a child through other agencies but they have not all found one. Some would-be adopters have reluctantly accepted the reason why we could not work with them and have come to terms with the fact that no one will place with a couple whose own children are in care, with a homeless family or a family heavily in debt, with two parents when only one wants to adopt, with a woman who has battered a child or with a man who has been convicted for molesting children or for repeated life-endangering driving offences. But we are hoping to place with another man who went through an anti-authority phase in his mid-twenties and collected several convictions for theft and unruly behaviour but has been a contented husband and father for the last twenty-five years. We have not placed with a young woman who has a terminal illness because she has not been told she has it and therefore it cannot be discussed with her, but we have placed with parents who are lame, diabetic, epileptic, and have had psychiatric illnesses. We are at present working with a husband who is partially sighted and a wife who is blind. The person who has been ill and found treatment and used it to get better or the person who is disabled and coping shows a healthy ability to overcome problems and we never look for people who have not had problems to face.

Although families usually counsel themselves out so that if six initially respond to the same child we are left with only one, there are times when we do have to choose. We can only share the reasons for the choice as we share the reasons for all decisions and most families go on to become interested in another child. But we cannot pretend that people are not disappointed and dejected when we do not give them the child they want; or when we also want them to have that child, and the local authority, in whose care the child remains until an adoption order is made, takes the decision out of our hands.

This happened with Ken and Scott, a homosexual couple with a stable and long-standing relationship. They had much experience of caring for mentally handicapped children. They had their own home and approving friends and relations. In our opinion they could have been excellent prospective parents for a severely retarded boy who had no preconceived ideas about families. The local authority felt unable to accept our view and Ken and Scott are still waiting for a child – but what is worse, the boy they hoped to have does not have parents. It was not suggested that homosexuals would corrupt a child, but it was feared that the establishment of the Council and the establishment of the Courts would not approve. The establishment has, after all, only just approved of single male parents as foster fathers and it is not yet easy for a single man to be accepted as an adoptive father even if he is not homosexual.

As we are working within a society where permanent families are no longer the norm, is it productive to be planning for permanence? When single parents are bringing up children successfully is it reasonable to turn down families because we fear the marriage might not last? Or might it be more important to feel confident that the partners of a marriage could survive a separation as parents. We have placed with two couples who have since divorced. One took us by complete surprise and we had to move Marion because she was not yet adopted and neither parent could cope with an emotionally distressed child on top of the destruction of the marriage. The other couple did not surprise us when the split came. They were honest about their positive relationship when we placed Keith and they were honest when the relationship deteriorated. Keith was adopted before the divorce; he lives with his mother and sister and sees his father and is incomparably better off than he was before he had a family. Of course he has suffered, but at least he knew why. Perhaps the very best we can do is to reintroduce children to the normal risks of family life and so prevent their isolation.

Sandra, the angry one, demanded that we find her a 'normal' family. She felt uneasy about her own outrageous behaviour and worried in case she was 'funny', and she did not want 'funny' parents either. It happened that the parents we first found for her were youngish, nice-looking, well off and totally committed to Sandra. But she literally kicked them in the teeth and ran and they remain scarred from their encounter with a child they wanted to cherish, but who would not let them. Sandra moved on quickly to the only family who we knew could hold on to her: a single mother with a caring friend and thirteen children at home. At least four others had grown up and left home already. Whenever we mention this family to people for the first time they dismiss it as 'just another kind of Children's Home'. When they visit and talk to the children and stay for a meal they know that it is just another kind of normal family.

10 Hello, Fay's Mummy – Introductions

We were warned that no family would be right for Fay and that introductions would have to be virtually under cover until she was as used to her would-be parents as to the residential workers with whom she felt safe. Fay, a twelve-year-old Down's syndrome child with little speech, did not feel safe with many people. Twice she had been introduced to couples who explained they were her new Mummy and Daddy, but she was still living in the Children's Home. The last Mummy and Daddy said 'see you next weekend' and never did. Fay could not understand that illness in the family prevented them from carrying out their plan. There was something unsettling about parents and they made her feel miserable and she did not want any more and managed to say so. When couples, any couples, came to visit the Children's Home, Fay pushed forward the first child she could grab hold of and shouted, 'Take her, not me, take her.'

We were somewhat daunted by our task and while Hilary worked with Fay's housemother to prepare Fay to try again I prepared her eager parents-to-be for a long and wearying introduction. Lily and Bob Dale were experienced parents. They had brought up five children on a farm labourer's income and it had not been easy for them but they had dealt with situations in a way that made us feel confident they could handle Fay who was nearing adolescence. They already had a younger Down's syndrome foster child and a Down's syndrome grandchild so that they knew more about the disability than we did. They were guided by the teachings of the Bible, they were at ease with themselves as parents and did not look for quick rewards from their children. They felt a great sympathy for Fay's reluctance to meet anybody at all and together

73

we worked out a series of casual, well spaced out visits.

The Dales were all set to wait for as long as it took Fay to accept them, but they were nervous when it was time for the first meeting. They arrived an hour early and had endless cups of tea in a nearby café. Then they went in one at a time so that Fay would not immediately identify them as a couple. They were pleased because Fay seemed to pay little attention when they each came in with a different member of staff. She did not really seem to notice them until they were sitting down side by side in the window seat. Then she came straight over to them and, without a moment's hesitation, said, 'Hello, Fay's Mummy, hello, Fay's Daddy,' and she plonked herself down between them.

We shall never know what went on in Fay's mind that day, because even if she knows she would never be able to explain anything so complicated. We do know that disguised introductions have a way of kidding no one but may ease the pressure on the child and possibly on the parents too. To her new parents' delight Fay attached herself to them from that day on and was ready to move within a month. The first time she went to stay with the Dales for a weekend on the farm they took her to see a pantomime in the nearby town. When the comic asked for children to come up on the stage to sing, Fay trundled up with the rest, but she tripped when she got down from the stage and while she struggled to regain her balance she screamed, 'Mummy!' piercingly, for the whole audience to hear. Her new mother is shy and blushed, but she also glowed with pride.

The course of introductions is as unpredictable in the adoption of older and handicapped children, as it is before marriage. We have evolved patterns that work, but we can only prepare children and parents for how we think it will be and outline a probable plan so that children, parents and workers do not feel even more threatened by the unknown. How must it be to look at each other that first time and wonder? More like an arranged marriage than a birth, yet we expect families to build up parent-child relationships and to compensate each other for all the growing together they have missed. It is frightening enough to be meeting strangers who want to be your parents or to meet a child already formed who is to become your son or daughter without the added strain of not knowing what will happen next.

It is easier for families to change provisional plans than to plan as they go along. So when children and parents are ready to meet we make an 'introductions plan'. We plan the first meeting in the minutest detail. 'Where' and 'when' are crucial. Time off from school is better than a tired fractious child and a short first meeting quickly followed by a leisurely weekend is better than a drawn out meeting followed by a long wait for the next one; and it is best to avoid the long summer holidays, which are a trial for most parents and children, for the start of a placement. It may be tempting to think that an extended holiday will give the family a chance to settle down together, but a difficult child without friends for twenty-four hours a day could be enough to break a family up.

Many children prefer the first meeting to take place on neutral ground and choose the Parents for Children office where all the work around adoption has been going on. Other children want the family to come and see them first where they live, especially if their Children's Home is geared towards adoption; but Sandra hated the idea of anyone coming to see her because she lived in a Home with tough adolescents who would laugh at her for wanting to have parents. Some older children have told us very firmly that the first meeting had to be at the parents' house because they wanted to look them and it over. Even the most handicapped children we have placed who have been unable to participate in the planning, have been aware of something special going on when they have met their parents.

First meetings are tense no matter where they take place, so it is as well to plan an activity like making the tea together, buying something from the shops, or just going for a drive and getting to know each other's landmarks. Picnics work well and our first farming family found it reassuring to prepare a huge pile of sandwiches, sausage rolls, cakes and drinks for their potential daughter and two sons who were renowned for their large appetites.

Not only 'where' and 'when' but 'who with' has to be carefully thought out. Children need to have the approval of the people they know and trust before they can risk new

attachments. We always try to make sure that the most significant adult in the child's life is present at that first meeting. Not
all the time, not so that they seem to be intruding, but so that
they can say to the child afterwards: 'I think this will be good
and right for you.' It is comforting for the child if this same
person can prepare them for the meeting, usually not more
than a day or two before, depending on the child's capacity to
hold on and for some children this is less than an hour! James'
devoted nursing sister told him as a matter of routine during
the normal fortnightly train journey to Parents for Children
that he was about to meet his new parents. Dawn was not told
until we were literally sitting down and waiting for the door-
bell to ring because we feared she would go to pieces if there
was a delay, but Hannah needed a whole week to adjust to the
very idea.

What do children want to know about families before they
meet them? Not what we would ask. Not 'who are they', 'what
do they do?' or 'how do they live and bring up their children?',
but 'do they have a car?' is often the first question. Many
children we have placed have easily come to terms with not
having a car, but it is one of the symbols of family life they
have been taught to recognise. 'Where will I sleep?' is near the
top of the list and not 'where do they live?' but 'how far away?'
Who wants to move far away from everything known, to take
what must always seem to be a leap in the dark? 'Where will I
go to school?', 'Do they have a dog, a cat, a baby, and other
children?' come in that order. Children do not really know
what to ask and this gives the would-be parents a valuable
opportunity to tell their own tale as they think their children-
to-be would like to learn it.

Belinda, Tony and Norman, the trio on the farm, were
given a life story book about their new family made by
their new mother and father, so that they would know them
before they met them: know all about the animals and the
house and see photos of their parents' wedding, of the grandparents and life on the farm and understand that there was
space for them. Jenny's family drew a tree with family photos
framed on every branch except one which had an empty frame
and said 'waiting for Jenny', and Emily's parents wrote and
illustrated a story about a Mummy and Daddy who longed for

a special little girl. Most families have made something for their child so that the first meeting is softened and enriched by what has already been exchanged. For the children know that the parents have also seen their photographs and been told their stories and very often children ask us to show the work they themselves have done to prepare for adoption. Perhaps what children really want to know is: 'Will they like me if they know me and is there room for me in their hearts as well as their lives and their homes?'

We make the introduction plan to cover everything from the details of the first meeting to the placement itself with all the visits and telephone calls and postcards in between. We try to predict how often parents and children will need to visit each other and at what intervals. We suggest that the child leaves some belongings in the new parents' home and we encourage the family to take responsibility for getting the child back to the Children's Home after each visit. Children feel more secure if they can see that their new family is in control and cares for their safe return and well being. If the parting is sad, it is better for the parents to have to travel home alone, than for an upset child to be taken away from them and carried off. Children in care have experience of being moved without very much preparation or explanation and it is reassuring if the parents can be seen to be in charge from the beginning.

We make sure that the times fit in with everyone, that transport will be available, that the workers the child needs will be involved and most important of all that no one will ever wonder when and where they will see each other again. 'We'll come again soon' is not at all the same thing as 'See you next Thursday after school outside the main gates.' Some of the children we place have bitter memories of adults who said 'See you next week' and did not. Two days of undefined waiting can seem like a life time to an uncertain child and a week like a life sentence.

To complete the introduction plan, we work in visits to schools and doctors and whatever else applies to this particular child and this particular family. And we allow time for feedback sessions. Regular interchange of feedback is essential between the child, the new family, the Children's Home or foster parents and the adoption agency. It is the only way we can all work towards the same end without misunderstandings and misconceptions. It is no good if the Children's Home does not know about the weekend visit and the family has no idea of what happened in the week. And it is no good at all if the adoption agency does not know what is going wrong as well as what went well.

Finally we add our own home phone numbers to the plan and type it on yellow paper and send copies to everyone concerned. We are told that parents live with the yellow plan throughout introductions. Mainly, we suspect, so that they know what they are changing, because the plan can only be provisional, can only offer a framework and it hardly ever remains unaltered. When it does we even perversely begin to wonder whether the family is as flexible and enterprising as we had hoped, but our fears on this score have been unfounded, and here, as in so many other aspects of adoption, we have learnt that one way may be as good as another. We believe that we do not have to understand everything as long as we can respond to what is happening.

Two nine-year-old girls lived in the same Children's Home and had a pretty similar experience of life. Both were referred to Parents for Children, both were introduced to two parents, comparable plans were made for both families, but we thought that stubborn Deirdre would take longer to make an attachment to her childless parents than Hannah, who was more pliable and longed for a baby which her new parents happened to have. Deirdre and her parents fell in love at first sight and Deirdre packed her case and begged to go home with them that very day and as they wanted her to come, there seemed little point in putting obstacles in the way. Of course, Deirdre had to go back again later, to the Children's Home, to say goodbye, to have a leaving party at school, to finish off one bit of life before starting another, but in her mind and in her parents' minds, she moved on that first day and the introduction plan flew out of a window. But Hannah was, after all, very cautious. She did not demur, hesitate or complain but she wanted to take it step by step just as planned and so did her parents. Both girls have been adopted for several years now. Deirdre is explosive, always in trouble and testing her parents to the limit; Hannah is contained, even aloof and always co-operative. Perhaps we did not know the children well enough, but children have a habit of not being themselves until they know where they belong.

In order to belong, children must move from the outside to the inside of the family circle, and introductions have to do with helping them on their way. Edward, who had a graphic turn of mind, was helped by actually drawing a circle with the members of the family inside it and himself on the outside. We asked whether the circle would open and he said yes, it opened every time his new single parent made the long journey to come and see him. Was it ever left open, we pursued, and was there room in it for anyone else? He thought there was plenty of room but said he could only get through the circle if his parent took him. His new mother did take him but Edward's understanding of his place in the family did not smooth the day to day rough edges of getting to know each other. During every visit he spread his six feet four inches all around the floor and certainly filled every space there was but he did nothing else. He did not allow himself to be involved with the family goings on, nor did he help or in any way visibly enjoy himself or otherwise, but with all his might, which was his height, he proclaimed that he was there.

There are many ways of moving into a family circle. Dawn broke into it, she was another child who needed to make everything into a battle. We even wondered whether we could safely place her with a family because Dawn, who looked like an angel, had some frightening habits like locking herself in her room in the Children's Home and pretending she was being beaten and yelling for help until, once, the police arrived. She met her match in her new father, Gordon Newsome, a policeman, who also liked a battle so that there were to be many of them in the years to come. But first they became allies against the rest of us and it bonded them together for ever.

Dawn met her parents on Good Friday and on Easter Sunday they collected her from the Children's Home and took her to visit their home. All according to plan. But on Sunday evening Dawn telephoned me at my home. She was not going back, she said, she liked it where she was. Her new father had gone on duty, but had said he wished she could stay and her new mother said yes so what was I going to do? Not much, late on Easter Sunday. I spoke to Iris Newsome and we agreed that Dawn had little to gain from being forced to go back and at twelve years old had much catching up to do on family life. I consulted with the parts of our team in London over the holiday, I spoke to the Children's Home staff and Dawn's own social worker who had also given her home number, and the placement was confirmed. The post mortem took longer and was after Easter, for people in high places were not impressed by the speed and co-ordination. 'Children are not placed like that,' said the Heads of Departments; but sometimes they are. When Dawn's father came off duty in the early hours of Easter Monday there was a message for him propped up on the television set. 'We've won Dad' was all it said and needed to say.

Unlike Edward, Sandra did not wait passively to be taken into the family circle nor did she break into it like Dawn. She resisted the idea of entering while demonstrating her terrible need with every unhappy word and action and in the end she had to be forced in. She saw the circle as graphically as Edward, without having to draw it. When she met the warm generous couple who wanted to become her parents, she would not walk with them and dragged five paces behind. When I took her to visit them she would not come into the house and sat outside on a bench by a telephone kiosk all on her own until the couple brought out the lunch and joined her as she refused to join them. Only by that time Sandra had rung the fire brigade and the lunch was interrupted and spoiled by the arrival of clanging engines and suspicious firemen.

Telephones played a hilarious part when Sandra was finally forced into her large, well prepared, one parent family circle. Her fighting spirit was renowned by then and we had made one of our very careful plans in order to avoid a shameful scene. For it is shameful if we allow a child like Sandra to threaten and intimidate and feel the utter loneliness that results from the fear that adults are not in control. Sandra had already broken my gear lever on a previous journey so this time we took no chances and ordered a hire car. We had to get the timing right so that there would be the minimum delay between Sandra's social worker telling her about the plan and putting it into effect. Her clothes and belongings had to be collected from the Children's Home after she had left so that the other teenagers would not gang up on her. I had to wait by a certain telephone box near the Home so that the house-mother could ring me the moment Sandra had left with her housefather to meet her social worker. This would give me only a few minutes to get her things and catch up with Sandra and her social worker and the hire car. A real cloak and dagger affair and we were edgy and apprehensive.

I arrived at the appointed place a good half hour early. One or two people used the telephone in the box but they did not make long calls. As it drew nearer to the agreed time for my call, I stood right by the box ready to stake my claim. At precisely the moment when I expected the phone to ring an engineer arrived, walked into the box and began to dismantle the phone. I demurred, he insisted, I became hysterical and said there was nothing wrong with the phone, he was irrita-tingly slow and patient and explained that the instrument was due for an overhaul and he would be at least half an hour. I pleaded, I even tried to let him into the cloak and dagger business but he thought I was mad. Then, while we were still gazing at each other in mutual disbelief, the assorted wires and screws which were all that was left of the telephone began to give an unmistakable ring. With wonderful good nature and a wicked grin the engineer pushed the bundle of wires back into something resembling a telephone receiver and handed it to me still ringing. I have no idea what else he did to make it stop ringing because there was nothing left to lift it off, but it worked and Sandra was on her way. I have never told Sandra this story, but I hope three years later, in the middle of her large family, it will make her laugh.

We are sometimes asked whether children tell us about the kind of family they want and whether we look for what they say. Generally children who can communicate – and not all the children we place can speak – tell us that they would like to live in something like Hollywood with a Rolls Royce forever at the door. Or in the Wild West on a horse, or with some family they have seen on television. Just occasionally a child makes a need known which we must take seriously. A desperately unhappy four-year-old told us in no uncertain terms and without words that he could not bear a rival and would do physical harm if one came his way. We did not place him in a family with younger children.

Hannah longed for a baby, but we did not try to find one for her. We did, however, find parents for her who just happened to have a baby and the baby was the making of that placement; for at least the parents, who were not to enjoy any rewards from Hannah for some time, could bask in the love and care their baby was being given. It was wonderous to see Hannah come home from school in the early days and without pause pick up the baby very gently and carefully and ask solicitously about every moment of her day. Without trying, babies and animals can achieve the simple and direct relationships with troubled children which may evade parents. The wise mother and father will allow and encourage their new child to confide in the dog, they will buy a coveted kitten or rabbit which can be loved and will turn a blind eye if the puppy is taken to bed, and they will even not mind too much if their precious baby is taken over, for a while, by their new daughter. In good time, the new child will feel secure enough to try out the new skill of loving and trusting on parents, but in the meantime it is safer with less powerful creatures.

Hannah really needed her baby, but Nick, who insisted that he must have brothers and sisters, now lives happily as a much loved and valued only child. He had to wait a long time for his parents because we also believed that he needed the more easy going atmosphere of a large family and we could not find one with space for Nick. In the end we were persuaded by a childless couple who are as easy going as any parents can be and yet have all the time in the world for a new son. Their introduction to each other was a period of practising.

We have to practise everything we want to learn to do well and becoming a family is no exception. Even just to say the words 'Mum and Dad' and 'my son' needs practice. To have a twelve-year-old son in the house when there's only been the two of you for fifteen years needs a lot of practice. To have the same two people with you all the time, caring, sharing, disciplining, cooking, shopping and sleeping needs some getting used to. To give physical affection and to allow physical closeness is very hard to learn. Nick and his parents did not hurry. They made some mistakes but you have to be able to make mistakes if you are practising. And they created a few family rituals to help them practise.

In biological families traditions grow up with the children, but when older children are adopted the rituals have to be invented. Nick's early childhood had been full of violence and as such children often do, he provoked violence in others. As soon as he met his new father Nick tried to make him use force. As soon as his new mother restrained him from some minor misdemeanour he tried to make her hit him. Nick had to learn that violence would not be used, that the parents would be in control without it and that physical contact can be non-violent. There developed, during the introductions, a family ritual of vigorous rough and tumble. Nick's father has been a soldier and knows something about physical combat and he impressed Nick with his ability to be strong without becoming violent.

Danny knew what kind of family he did not want. He was on the verge of being in trouble with the law and he did not want a copper for a dad. Yet strangely a policeman is what he got because his policeman father was attracted by Danny's likeness to himself as an adolescent. He was exactly the right person to help Danny conquer his fear of the law and stay on the right side of it. But it took a lot of practice while they got to know each other.

Practising goes on when children move in for good with their new families especially if the habit has been formed during introductions. Each step in the adoption process is a continuation of the last one and the success of the way forward will always depend on the foundations laid behind. There is no division between birth and growing up and there is no division between introductions and placement and legal adoption and post-adoption living; it is all just another way of building a family – not by birth but by adoption.

But introductions do not always lead to placement and sometimes it is necessary to take a step back before moving forward again. James' first introductions were too painful for everybody and we should have stopped them after the first meeting but it is tempting to hope that after all the work put in, things must get better. The parents were so anxious to compensate their own two girls for the strange child they wanted to adopt that they could hardly see James. Their children arrived with shiny new toys and they had all of their parents' attention. James sat wide eyed and empty handed surveying the family scene. It could not work, but until that moment the parents had not known how they would feel and neither had we.

The last word on introductions must be Guy's. He was three years old when we placed him with a childless couple. For babies and toddlers we usually plan very short and very intensive introductions. Guy's parents came to stay near his foster home and visited daily until they were virtually looking after him and he was relaxed with them. Although Guy was a bright, sturdy toddler, he was small for his age because he is an achondroplasic child who will not reach a normal height. He had had some problem with hearing and speech and we were not at all sure how much he understood of what was going on. He moved easily to his new home and become a contented boy with an endearing personality and an enquiring mind. He learned to speak well enough and his hearing improved, but he did not seem to remember anything at all about his introduction and placement. Then one day, his father took out a pair of shoes he had not worn for years and with some surprise, but no hesitation, Guy said, 'Those are the shoes you wore when you used to come and see me at Auntie Joy's before you took me home.' A child's eye view which we must not forget.

SOME PARENTS FOR CHILDREN FAMILIES

Photo Ingrid Darracott

Photos Ingrid Darracott

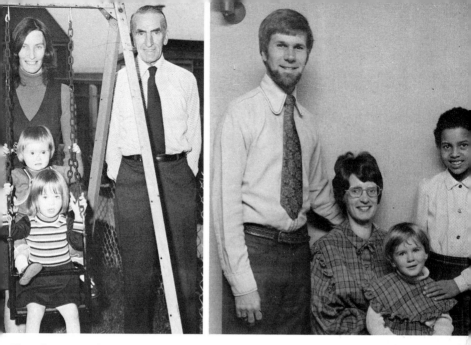

Photo Community Care

Photo *Woman,* Syndication International Ltd

Photo Glendale Studios, Tadley

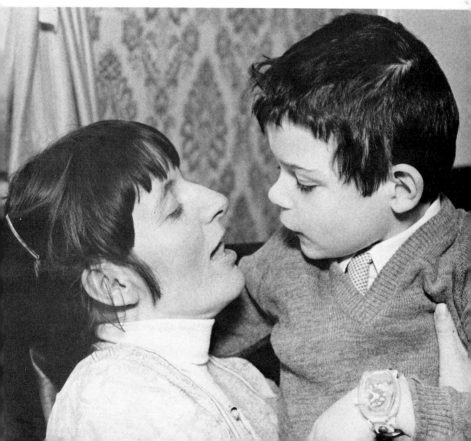

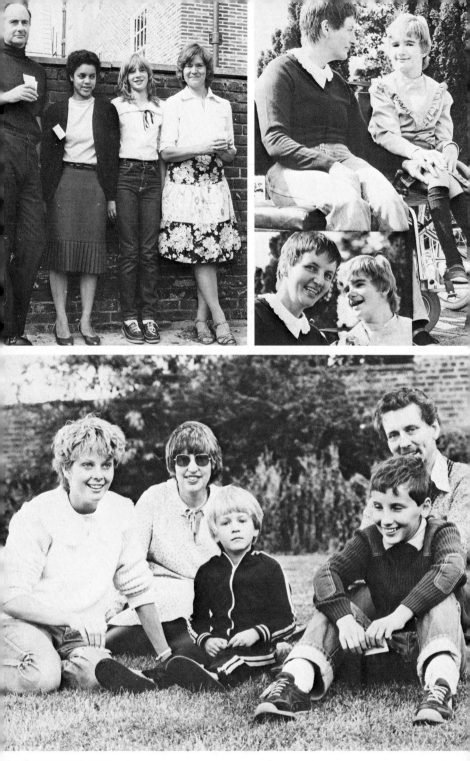

Photos Ingrid Darracott

Photo Ingrid Darracott
Photo Coe Colour Centre, Norwich

Photo *Evening Echo*

Photo *Daily Mail*

Photo *Woman's Own,*
Syndication International Ltd

Publicity by courtesy of Geo.
Bassett & Co. Ltd

Four Powerful Women?

Left: 222, Camden High Street.

Right: The room downstairs.

Below left: Sue and Katina at the Centre. Photos Ingrid Darracott

Below right: Pages from James' life story book. Photo Community Care

In 1979 when I was 5 years old we went to wales for the summer. Vivienne and Martine took Jeff and me with Topsy the dog. We stayed in a caravan on Betty's farm. We learnt to milk the cows and the goats. I also drove a tractor and rode a horse called Amber.

In 1980 we went back to wales and took Tracy as well this time. Amber has had a foal called Bracken.

Betty has a husband called Frank and two children called Stephen and Stan. Stan is a girl.

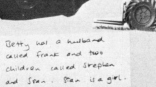

FAMILIES AND HELPERS AT THE ANNUAL PARENTS FOR CHILDREN PICNIC

Photos Ingrid Darracott

Photos Ingrid Darracott

Photos Ingrid Darracott

Photos Ingrid Darracott

Photos Ingrid Darracott

Sheeraz with her new mother. Photo Sally and Richard Greenhill

11   The Caretakers

How do foster parents and residential workers feel when we take away a child? We talk about the needs of the child in adoption and we constantly ask ourselves how does it feel? How does it feel to be neglected or unwanted, to live in an institution, to be fostered, to be parentless, to have a social worker, to be featured in publicity, to be introduced to a family, to be adopted?

We pay attention to the adopters. We appreciate their strengths and do not want to undermine their weaknesses. We regard them as individuals, try to meet their own special needs, and cherish what they have to offer. But what about the caretakers? The people who are taking care of the child in the meantime, who usually know the children best, who stay up at nights when they are sick, who deal with their day to day joys and aggravations and have to take some responsibility for bringing them up?

Residential social workers have chosen a job with unsocial hours and not enough pay in order to take care of other people's children. Foster parents allow themselves to love a child who will leave them. Nursing and medical staff in subnormality hospitals have the thankless task of caring for the most handicapped children and workers in specialised schools and residential communities concentrate all their skills on treating the emotionally damaged child. How do all of them feel when we come along and say thank you very much and now we are going to find something better?

Naturally the caretakers also want the best for the child and will have been included in the decision that a child needs a family, but the decision itself must surely feel like a criticism of their caring or an undervaluing of what they have given. If a

Home for disabled children offers the best and most up to date
aids to living, how can a family offer more? In residential
treatment settings there must often be a niggling feeling
among the workers that more could be done, that the child is
not quite ready, that a family will not be able to carry on the
good work. One housemistress in a therapeutic boarding
school cannot accept that a girl she had struggled to change
for six years is doing better with her single parent. She
regularly accuses us of not understanding the psychodynamics
of childhood and change and charges us with a belief in magic.
We do not believe in magic, but we do know that children
change magically when they have their own family. Even their
appearance changes; they look more vital: their hair begins to
shine and their skin to glow.

I fear that in our enthusiasm and our determination to find
the right family for each child we do not always give due
weight to the feelings of the caretakers. Our message seems
loud and clear: 'anything you can do, they may not do better
or as well, but it will be best for this child'; and 'they' are all the
untrained and possibly inexperienced and in fact quite
average people who become parents. A depressing message for
women and men who struggle daily within bureaucratic
systems to devote their lives to 'child care'. And it is a message
in which we wholeheartedly believe.

Not that all caretakers feel slighted when we take children
away from them and place them for adoption. The majority
support the plan and believe it to be in the best interests of the
child. But we do not make it easy for them because all of us
social workers do not concern ourselves often enough with the
nature of residential care and foster care and we are too vague
about the reason and aims for each such placement. If the
child cannot return to natural parents does the child need
stand-in parents, supplementary parents or permanent substitute parents? Or how and why would the child's needs be met
by residential treatment in a Children's Home? And how can
we expect residential social workers to give children the loving
and caring they demand without becoming substitute parents
themselves? Or how can we expect foster parents to hold on
one day and let go the next? If we stand by while children
and their caretakers get along as best they can from one six

monthly review to the next, and we either avoid making long term plans or do not see them through, then we should not be surprised when houseparents and foster parents are not prepared for adoption.

One short term foster mother was horrified when we found a family to adopt her Down's syndrome foster baby within a month of being asked. She had agreed that the baby should be adopted but she was not used to that kind of decision being carried out. Her previous Down's syndrome foster baby to be adopted was now seven years old and still with her.

Adoptive parents hardly ever come up to the caretaker's expectations. Foster parents tend to hope for a family just like themselves because if the child has been happy with them, they want him to be able to repeat the experience and the child tends to want the same. So that Nick wanted a large family because he spent his holidays from boarding school with a foster Mum and Dad and their seven children and he could not think of anything better. An elderly foster mother with grown up sons and daughters may find it unbearable to know that the disabled baby she has nurtured is going to a family where it will have to find its place among the hurly burly of five other small brothers and sisters. Residential social workers who are exhausted although they work prescribed hours and go off duty cannot easily accept that a woman will take on their most difficult child single handed and without a salary. We have to remind the caretakers as we have to remind ourselves, many times, that we and they are not adopting and that parents do not compete with their skills because parents do something entirely different.

It took many highly qualified people to look after Robin in hospital. He is severely subnormal, blind, spastic and epileptic. He will never walk unaided or talk with words. He was tended day and night by psychotherapists, occupational therapists, doctors, psychiatrists, special teachers and nurses. His single mother-to-be was a slight, shy young woman, unused to stating her case. Without malice and with kindly intentions, she was scrutinised and interrogated every time she visited, every time she touched Robin and every time she took him out of the safety of the hospital grounds. Perhaps it strengthened her to have to fight for her disabled son from the very beginning, but there are gentler ways to help a single parent to gather her strength.

Robin was five years old and had had thirty-seven care-takers by the time he was adopted. It is not an easy job to be a special nurse in the children's ward of a subnormality hospital and when nurses come, from many different countries, they do not stay long. Robin heard twelve different languages during the time other children learn to speak. He seemed not to differentiate between caretakers, let alone to relate to them. And how could the changing caretakers and cor-poration of experts relate to the adoption plan? Each time the new mother collected Robin a different Sister was on duty, each time she brought him back the shift had changed. Some-times some of the experts were present and available and sometimes they were not. No one could ever tell her all she wanted to know, not about his medical condition, but about his behaviour and response between her visits and there was no one person to monitor the progress she and Robin were making together. In the end, the local authority social workers and Parents for Children decided by remote control that Robin was ready to leave the hospital and he did. Of all the children we have placed Robin had the least consistent good caretaking, though he needed it most, but the expert care-takers all round him put up the greatest resistance to handing over responsibility.

It is all to do with the handing over of day to day responsi-bility. To begin with the caretakers have it all and during introductions they must pass it over, bit by bit to the new parents. Foster parents are asked to hand over responsibility in their own homes to adopters meeting a very young child. It must be excruciating for an experienced foster parent to watch a new mother who is probably almost paralysed with nerves. One wise foster mother left the baby and her home to the new parents as soon as she was confident that the child was not going to come to harm. She enjoyed her few days of freedom while new parents and child got to know each other and she wept when the family left, but she had handed over responsibility fully and gladly for the child's sake and said that it did not at all feel like her baby going because she could already feel that he was theirs.

Adopters have told us that the hardest part of adoption is visiting a Children's Home. Even when they have got on well with the staff and have liked what they have seen, it has been an uncomfortable experience for them. They have not been able to rid themselves of the feeling that they were intruding into an alien culture and disrupting the routine and therefore the lives of the residents. It is hard for institutions to adapt to visitors and in some residential homes visiting families have not been offered a cup of tea after a lengthy journey because it was not tea-time. The staff were not being rude and would certainly have offered the same families a cup of tea in their own homes, but somehow the life of an institution can displace the ordinary rules of hospitality. Even if there is a welcome with tea and home made cakes there is still the unease. Perhaps this is because it is too difficult for parents to assume responsibility in the Home for their child-to-be and too difficult for staff to hand it to them in an environment which they control. When tea time finally comes and the child messes his food, the residential worker is unable to let the parents take charge and disciplines him without a second thought, and it is the parents who are then left, metaphorically, with the egg on their face.

Caretakers can sabotage a placement without much effort. The child needs their approval to make a move and approval can be withheld in all kinds of ways. Damaging remarks about the prospective parents can completely undermine a child's precarious ability to trust. Charles at fourteen was scared by his own sexual development and aggressive feelings, although he liked to give the impression that he was a man of the world. He ate too much and was worried about being laughed at by girls because he was big and broad for his age. His brother Gerald was ten and still very much a little boy. They lived in a small Children's Home with two houseparents who truly believed that the children were happy where they were and that they should stay. These caretakers were mystified and resentful when the decision was made to find an adoptive family for Charles and Gerald and they could not have approved of anyone who turned up. Unfortunately they chose their battleground well. They began to make fun of the would-be father because he was overweight and they developed the notion that he looked at them in a strange way. Their jokes turned the introductions sour for Charles because they took him into the very area he could not handle. While Gerald remained unconcerned by the jokes and became more and more attached to the family, Charles drew further and further away. In the end, the brothers who had asked to remain together, chose to separate; Gerald wanted his family at all costs and Charles could not accept this family at any cost. Gerald was adopted and Charles remained hovering outside the family circle, sometimes visiting, sometimes writing and sometimes refusing to have any contact at all. By the time he was sixteen he was in regular trouble with the police and had to leave the Children's Home for a detention centre.

Not every negative intervention from caretakers is as dramatic. There are many ways of disapproving. One foster mother did not choose to tell us that she regularly sedated the Down's syndrome baby she cared for. When this baby moved to his adoptive home he screamed day and night and made his new parents frantic. They knew he had been a contented baby in the foster home and they feared that they were bad for him and gave up. We went back to the foster mother and found out about the sedatives, but by this time we had had to move the baby. At least we could tell his next family the whole story and this baby is now an extremely healthy and lively little boy who sleeps all night without sedation and plays all day.

Then there are the subtle ways in which caretakers can put obstacles in the way. The parents arrive at the Children's Home and the child is not there. The visit has not been put down in the diary or the diary has been mislaid and the child has been taken on an outing. Or the caretaker has forgotten to pack the wellingtons for a country weekend. Or the child has an appointment with the paediatrician or an assessment at school and someone has forgotten to invite the new parents-to-be. This is a sad list and when anything like it happens we must look at why it is happening, because if we are not taking the caretakers with us we are putting the adoption plan in jeopardy.

There is one further complication. Children have a disconcerting habit of not behaving at all in the same way with two different sets of people. So that residential workers may warn parents of some behaviour problem which will never happen. Or parents will describe a worrying habit which the foster mother has never seen. This does not exactly encourage trust and we have known parents complain that the caretakers do not know their child and caretakers have made noises about families who do not understand their children. Even when children behave in exactly the same way wherever they are, the same behaviour may have very different results.

Thelma, the fifteen-year-old multiply handicapped girl who disliked babies, had a habit of emptying out all the drawers in her Children's Home. None of the drawers were private – the staff lived elsewhere, and no one possessed anything of value – so that it was more peaceful for the caretakers to let Thelma get on with it. When Thelma went to visit the family we found for her, the housemother told them that Thelma loved emptying out drawers and this sounded harmless enough until it happened and then the parents were appalled. Documents, clothes, cutlery and photographs tumbled out in heaps and were shoved back any old how because Thelma always insisted on putting things back. Behaviour that was bearable in 'The Home' became quite intolerable in 'a home' and it left adopters and caretakers bewildered by each other's apparent misunderstanding of the problem. It seems that behaviour has to be translated from one situation to another, because rules, demands and aspirations can be so different as to render mere description meaningless.

Children have a hard enough time during introductions without being caught up in tension between old caretakers and new family. They need all the support they can get from both sides to make the transition a good experience. Most children like their foster homes and Children's Homes and the people in them and it does not help if families give the children the impression that they are being rescued. Even if the Children's Home has been pretty unsatisfactory, it has been important to the child, just as biological families are important even if they have abused their children. Feelings can be very mixed; fear of a natural father will not displace admiration for him and resentment of a housemother because she is paid to give a cuddle will not displace affection. Children need to be allowed to feel sad about what they are losing even if it was not good enough and their loyalty to caretakers and natural parents should not be undermined.

If Caretakers are the most significant people during a child's introductions and move to a new family, then the foster parents need support so that they have the time to concentrate on the handover; and in order for residential workers to be fully involved inside and outside the Home, someone in charge must be ready to give priority to an adoption placement.

Peter lived in a large Home which was subdivided into groups of eight children with their own houseparents when a new superintendent took over. The staff were trained and encouraged to insist on residential care with a purpose and on long term plans for each child in their charge. When they considered Peter they almost despaired: born with Down's syndrome, rejected at birth, placed with foster parents twice in his first year and written off as unfit for family life for the next seven. Everyone liked Peter, and everyone thought he should have a family; they only feared that the risk of another rejection was too great. But in the end he was referred to Parents for Children, and his preparation, introductions and placement were made a priority for his group.

Val was Peter's housemother and she was given all the time Peter needed. Time to bring him to Parents for Children, because although Peter could not speak he could understand about all the children who needed Mothers and Fathers. Time to make a poster with him which made Peter proud and a picture-book with photographs of all his friends, his school and the adults he had known. Time to carry out the immediate goal of teaching Peter the Makaton sign language and to prepare him for a move away from the only home he could remember. Time to prepare herself for handing over Peter to a stranger. Time to share her work with the rest of the group and to prepare them also for Peter's leaving. Time, when his single mother was found, to make the three hour journey each way with him every weekend for two months and, towards the end, when she was leaving Peter and collecting him again, time to make that same journey four times a week for we had found a parent who could not easily travel. All along Val's colleagues supported her, did not resent the extra work left for them although it meant constant rearranging of rotas, and finally rejoiced with her because it was a job exceptionally well done. And Val felt rewarded because Peter's successful placement for adoption was largely due to her good practice.

We cannot always expect or even hope that caretakers will be able to make a commitment like Val, because, on the whole, institutions are not geared to spare a member of staff frequently and for long periods. But many caretakers manage to see a child into placement in spite of organisational difficulties and if they are involved every step of the way they are more likely to feel that it is worth the effort. Like Val, all caretakers should know that their role is vital for the child and the child's new family and that adoption can be the crown of their work rather than a thorn in their side.

When it is all over, when the child has moved to a new family, the caretaker's part is not finished but we have come to recognise that it is often cut short at this point because it can be too painful to continue. It is perhaps enough to have survived the parting. Ideally the newly placed child needs to keep in touch, for a short time at least, with his previous caretakers. It is important to know that one does not have to lose one set of people when one gains another. But it rarely works out that way and it is not only the caretakers' predicament. Adopters find it hard, once the child is theirs, to maintain the contact. They do not want to upset their child and they know that the past was upsetting. They do not want to share their child, and although they are usually full of good intentions and make some effort to keep in touch with caretakers, their heart is not in it and the relationship fades too soon. There are as always notable exceptions; one residential worker has become the child's godmother and we are particularly impressed by the ex-foster mother who regularly looks after her ex-Down's syndrome foster child and all the other children of the family while the parents have a well deserved holiday. She has not lost a foster baby, she has gained three grandchildren and she is the kind of grandmother every child wants to have. But more often, foster homes and Children's Homes and all institutions are pressed to fill the space as soon as the child has gone. They may be able to hold the place for a few weeks until the child has settled, but soon another child's needs will be urgent and the caretakers will become concerned with the new arrival and the gap will close over.

12   Commitment

'They wanted a little girl and they wanted to make me into their little girl but I can't be, I'm me.' This was Sandra, raging against the foster parents who had tried for six years to mould her into the daughter they never had and who could not accept her as the child she already was. They were kindly, well-intentioned people and they hoped that in time Sandra would change and then they would adopt her. But time was against them for as it passed Sandra changed from a cuddly, wide-eyed distrustful five-year-old to a disruptive, deceitful, pubertal eleven-year-old. And then it was too late because by then Sandra felt so apart from the rest of the family that she had to test them to see how much she belonged. She ran away and was brought back and ran again and they let her go. But the single mother Sandra has now, has signed the contract which promises that no matter how often or how far Sandra runs, she will be brought back because this is where she belongs. A total commitment made in response to the child's need and in the belief that love can grow and in the hope that it will and in the knowledge that it may not.

Hannah's adoptive father is a clergyman. Long before love came a declaration from the pulpit: Hannah's father-to-be publicly announced to his congregation that a new daughter was joining his family and when she came she was immediately introduced as 'our eldest daughter, Hannah'. 'Commit and be blessed,' we said. Hannah, who was ten when she went to live in the rectory, was polite and good. Too much so it seemed to her new parents who felt concerned about her flat emotions. She was never angry, hardly ever excited, and almost never affectionate except towards her new baby sister, on whom she lavished all the feelings she could not show anyone else. A clever child, who could not concentrate, remember or, so it seemed at times, even hear. She could not learn at school in spite of all the help she had from her teacher mother and she covered up whatever she feared she had got wrong by telling lies. Not mean or nasty lies, but the first thing she could think of to get her out of trouble, like 'The teacher wasn't there today' when she forgot to give in the dinner money, or even 'I didn't want any dinner'. 'We don't have any homework' when she had left it at school and 'My friend's mother won't let her come to tea' because she did not have the courage to ask her friend. Hannah would say anything to avoid a confrontation and she was always surprised and panic stricken when found out, for lying was not treated lightly in that household. Nor was it easy to live with a child who gave little and took less, But even though Hannah did not feel as if she was their daughter, her parents knew that she was and so did Hannah. She never doubted for a moment that after three Children's Homes and three foster placements this was to be her real family. Not because she and her parents had fallen in love but because the commitment was acknowledged and renewed daily as they went about their lives. That is how most children live with their families. A child like Hannah may have to ask herself, 'Do they love me, do I love them?' but she should never have to ask 'Do they want me?'

If love can grow, can commitment grow also? Can parents and children afford to wait for it to grow? We were uncomfortable when Peter's mother took nearly two years to adopt him. She could only explain that she was not ready. We feared we had made a mistake, that this placement would drift on without commitment and break if Peter stopped making progress. We almost got to the point of moving him to another family. Our anxiety nearly prevented us from giving his mother enough space and time to make her own commitment in her own way. A way that was fine for Peter, but might not have suited a more able and comprehending child, but then it was Peter and not another child she was striving to make her own. The line between trying to change children to make them acceptable, and adjusting to make the child one's own is a fine one and not always discernible to the outsider's eye.

We know now that Peter's mother has made as strong a

commitment to Peter as we could wish and that he will grow up within a caring family with every opportunity to develop and that she will fight for his rights as a Down's syndrome person; but we are still uncomfortable whenever parents treat the beginning of a placement like a trial period even if they do not call it that.

We are also uncomfortable about any proposal to place children for an initial period of foster care, if adoption is what both parents and child want and need. It does not seem helpful or sensible to make foster care, which is one thing, into a testing time for adoption which is another. We would rather have the testing time for thinking and preparing before introductions begin.

We agreed to place Nick with parents who would not insist on adoption because Nick's biological family was still very much on his mind. But as soon as a family was found Nick made it quite clear that he wanted to be adopted as quickly as possible. It is easier for a teenager to say that he does not want to be adopted than to admit that he does not believe any family will want him enough to make that kind of commitment.

Does commitment have a breaking point? James' second parents-to-be were committed enough to shelve their plans for a baby and move house and we were as confident about this placement as they were. Sandra's prospective adopters committed themselves so fiercely that we were persuaded against our better judgement to go ahead. Against our better judgement because we knew that Sandra could be damaging and we feared that these parents would be vulnerable. The one placement disrupted and the other one never got under way. Both families had much to offer and are now giving it to other children. Both children had great needs which are now being met elsewhere. We cannot know exactly how or why commitment gives way to disillusionment, regret and bitterness. We do know that the very qualities that make people hang on can also make them let go. The man who wanted to be Sandra's father is a successful business man and a happy husband but he has first hand knowledge of being uprooted, of separation and loss and of being the outsider. He had a deep understanding of Sandra's aggressive response to her own situation; but when he began to witness her hateful feelings acted out in physical attacks on his wife he could not go on, he had to protect his wife from destruction. Yet with the mixture shaken up just a little differently it could have worked.

Gordon Newsome is himself adopted, but did not know it until he applied to join the police force. He knows about the search for identity and later for natural parents. His alliance with Dawn is a stronghold from which she can venture out to meet the rest of the world. But Dawn might have unbalanced his own hard won security and it might not have worked. Or Gordon's wife, Iris, might not have been able to tolerate the alliance and to stand by until Dawn could include her. Dawn learned to cry and one day she sobbed in Iris' arms because she had had to wait all these years to find a mother. Why couldn't they have known about each other long ago, she wanted to know, it wasn't fair that they had missed so much, when all the time they had lived only a stone's throw apart. Iris and Dawn set forth to catch up with each other. They shared their grief at their loss of mothering and being mothered and they recreated for themselves the intimate world of mother and daughter from the beginning. Iris found the dolls' cradle from her own childhood which she had saved for a daughter but the daughter she had given birth to had not lived. They bought a doll and made dolls' clothes and played, giving each other what both had missed. Although Dawn was nearly thirteen they could do it for each other's sake. A whole-hearted commitment, a strong foundation, but yet there was a long way to go and it took a growing mutual love to overcome what Dawn could drag up from the depths of her own hurt. Like when she stood on top of the stairs one day, feeling miserable because she had behaved badly and been sent to her room, and she yelled at her mother, 'Why don't you use the money you spend on me to buy that brat who died a tombstone?' It takes everything there is to withstand that.

We used to think that there were certain things parents and children could not, must not say to each other and that the family would not survive if they did. That is why we hesitated before placing Dawn with the Newsomes; she had to make a remark like that sooner or later and in our book it was one of the things that could not be said. The Newsomes persuaded us that they could handle it and they did. There was still one thing though, that we felt should never be said. However hard parents were pushed, however desperate and angry, however hurt and disappointed, they must never threaten their child with 'I'll send you back'. We considered it the unforgivable sin in adoption and always said so to would-be parents. Worse than threatening home grown children with the bogey man because most children have a well founded suspicion that the policeman, the dustman and the man down the road do not really collect little girls and boys, but children in care know well about the reality of being sent back. We still insist that it cannot be good to make such threats but we know that such threats are made and that families have survived them. They have even told us that it cleared the air once the unspeakable was spoken. We would not advocate it as a method of disciplining, not even as a last resort, but we no longer believe that anything is beyond repair as long as there is enough commitment to carry on.

Very often parents use the opposite of the 'I'll send you back' threat with good effect. When the child has tried them beyond the limits of endurance, they will say firmly or shout wildly, depending on their individual inclination, 'It doesn't matter what you do, you're here to stay, so you may as well give up, belt up or simmer down.'

Then there is the child who is always threatening to go back herself. Jenny kept packing her case and taking it to the front door. For weeks the parents restrained themselves from saying, 'Well go then,' and did the right thing and reassured her each time that she was wanted and helped her to unpack again. Finally their patience snapped and after yet another temper tantrum they packed her case for her, wordlessly and put it by the front door. That was the end of the 'I'm going back' game and Jenny became more rather than less secure.

Not all natural parents love all their children all the time in the same way, but unless something goes wrong they are committed to their children. Adoptive parents of older children have to find ways to develop that commitment. They have to mark their child, to make it theirs through practice. Children and parents have to claim each other. The best we can do is to pass on to one family what we have learnt from another. Families are wonderfully inventive, probably because they are driven by necessity in order to survive.

Hannah's parents wanted to help her over the hurdle of touching. Hannah did not like being touched by anyone except the baby and she never put out her own hand. Her mother and father did not know why and were careful not to invade her defences but they explained to her that they liked touching when they felt loving. They did not hug her indiscriminately or as a matter of routine, and always said something caring before they gave her a pat on the shoulder, a stroke of the hair or a light kiss goodbye, nothing more. Then as Hannah became more physically receptive they suggested to her that she could also practise touching and they would remind her at certain moments in the day. Once, when Hannah was going to bed and her mother reminded her to say goodnight to her father, she asked the question which gave the key: 'How can I love you when I have to love my real Mummy and Daddy?' She had to have permission to love again and she had to have permission to remain loyal to the memory of her birth parents and they gave her both. Hannah needed more help to come and join the Saturday morning romp in her parents' bed. She felt too threatened even to go into the room until her parents gave her the privilege as eldest daughter of making the morning tea. At first she carried it in shyly and dumped it and ran. But after a few weeks she stayed longer and watched curiously while her little sister shouted and gurgled with excited delight at being tickled and rolled and bounced on the bed. Much later she joined in the fun and eventually found her own level and crept into her parents' bed for a Saturday morning read and a cuddle.

Other children, with Hannah's experiences of change and loss, crave physical reassurance and will take it indiscriminately from whoever will offer. Emily's parents had to accept that their precious adopted four-year-old would hurl herself at anyone. If she fell over she would as soon go to the nearest adult for comfort as seek out her mother. If visitors came she would climb up on their lap or go off for a walk with them without a backward glance. She couldn't even give her parents a special smile, because Emily has a paralysed face caused by Moebius' syndrome and cannot smile at all.

When children are born they learn first of all to relate to their mother, if their mother is available, and by putting all their good and bad feelings into her, make themselves feel safe and comfortable. Slowly, as they awaken to the immediate world around them, they see there are other special people whom they can trust to hold their feelings. As babies grow and become stronger they become more daring and they begin to explore relationships outside the family and sometimes their feelings get hurt. In this way children learn to differentiate between themselves, the family and the rest of the world. They discover that some people are vital for their survival and some people are not. That affection and anger have their place. And all that discovery makes very small children feel in control. They are magicians; they make the world go round. A good way to start life and a good foundation for becoming a responsible person.

Emily spent her infancy in the nursery spreading her feelings around in the hope of finding that special person who was not there and all the other special ones who did not come. Most of her feelings were lost as nursery nurses came and went and she learned that life was easier if feelings were not deep. When Emily finally got a family of her own she went on frantically spreading her feelings between as many people as she could because she feared that if all her feelings were lost, she would be lost too. She did not understand that it was safe for her to love and hate at last. And she did not know about being a magician. In fact she hardly realised that she was a separate person because she did not seem to have any control over her life at all and she felt as though everyone else was making her behave the way she did. So that she always said 'You made me do that' and 'It wasn't my fault'. Emily only really claimed her family when her baby sister was born. Through the baby she learned that her parents are the special people she had been looking for. She identified with the baby, she wanted to do everything the baby did and have everything the baby had and her sensitive parents let her, because they knew it was the only way she could claim them. Emily watches the baby's face as it wreathes into a smile. She looks earnestly at her mother and reassures her: 'I'm smiling too,' she says.

Often, when a baby is born into the family, the parents of an adopted child will become intensely conscious of all the good things the baby is having and their adopted child did not have. The adopted child of whatever age will also be watching and wondering. Parents have taken many opportunities to back track with a child that was not born to them. Not only by letting them relive their babyhood like Emily, but by filling in the gaps, sometimes with truth sometimes with fantasy, always with the desire to mark the child as a full member of the family.

When Hannah's young sister started school at four, Hannah was amazed by the fuss and the occasion that was made of it. Next day she got up earlier than usual for breakfast and she wanted to know, 'What do you "think" happened on my first day at school?' Not 'what happened?' – she was quite satisfied with a claiming story which would allow her to share her first day at school six years ago with her family now.

Some parents make up 'cover stories' to help them claim their children. Not to cover up something nasty or best forgotten, but to give their children cover and protection. Children need help to explain themselves. They should not have to tell everyone who asks their whole story; they have a right to feel that their new family holds their past for them and that it has become a private family matter. Dawn was relieved and proud when she could go to her new school and say, 'My Dad was adopted and so my Mum and Dad wanted to adopt me.' Just the implication that adoption was a good thing was enough to satisfy her school fellows and it made Dawn feel closer to her parents.

Margery, in the wheelchair, had her story pat and loved to tell it just as her new mother told it her. 'Why did you choose me?' asked Margery one day and her mother said: 'There were so many children needing parents, so I picked the only one who couldn't walk.'

Adoption is a commitment but very young children have difficulty understanding the whole idea of adoption. Belinda, Tony and Norman were too young to remember much before the farm. Their parents showed them adoption when it was lambing time. They took them out to the fields where the lambs were being born. They watched as the new lambs got up, shook themselves and nuzzled the ewes. But there were a few very young ones who did not seem to know about their lambs. They ignored them, they pushed them away when they tried to feed and they ambled off to feed themselves, leaving their lambs behind them. The three children helped to gather up the abandoned lambs and took them into the kitchen and put them in the warm in front of the wood burner and fed them watered down milk from a bottle. The parents explained that some ewes were not old enough or strong enough or experienced enough to look after their lambs and that the kitchen was a bit like a Children's Home for them.

Later the farmer and his wife and their children took the parentless lambs out one by one, to find them a substitute family. They looked for ewes which were already being good parents and they looked for ewes whose own lambs had died and who were pining to have another. They introduced the new lambs carefully and they played at being adoption workers while they watched and waited. They were overjoyed when a lamb and a ewe took to each other and sad if they did not, but they kept on trying until it worked. This is a favourite Parents for Children story which has helped many other parents and children far from farms and lambing time. It has been quoted by Jane Rowe in her book *Yours By Choice* and we are proud that one of our families created it. In the meantime Belinda, Tony and Norman patiently explain adoption to their friends and know that it is something they have seen and felt and shared with their parents.

Adopted children do not look like their new parents or sisters and brothers. At least there is no genetic inheritance of features, colouring and stature, so that to discover a likeness, or to create a similarity, is proof of commitment. It is amazing how many adopted children seem to grow to resemble their families or how many adoptive parents seem to transform themselves to resemble their child. One single parent who has adopted two very different children has managed to look like both of them. Margery's mother even looks like her first mother who died. Harry and his father are unmistakably father and son and Josephine is the spitting image of her adoptive mother's oldest daughter at the same age. If physical similarities are impossible to achieve or imagine, adoptive parents and children will find or forge other familial links in their effort to commit themselves to each other: a sense of humour like Aunt Harriet's or a temper like Uncle George's, having a mind for maths like Mum or being clumsy like Dad are the bonds which tie new families together.

When I was a social work student, my supervisor told me that you can always tell a good substitute family because they will fight for their child. I have remembered that whenever parents first stand by their child and face the world for him. Like Eric and Hilda and Mickey. Mickey was the fourteen-year-old son they first saw in a popular newspaper. He was not able to tolerate frustration and at school he hit out at teachers and boys alike. He did not hit out at home and Eric and Hilda knew that all he needed to calm him down was the attention and approval he craved. They tried to explain this to his teachers and they tried to help Mickey to control himself by making him believe that they cared and minded about him all the time he was away from them.

Eric took to working nights so that he could be around in the day, ready to go up to the school to sort things out for Mickey, ready to stand by him when he was in trouble. There was the time Mickey flatly refused to do needlework because, he said, it was sissy, and the school called Eric for he had asked to be called before violence happened. Eric advised Mickey to get on with his stitching because all the lads in the forces were doing the same and Mickey saw the sense in that because he wants to join the Army.

Mickey improved. There were not as many scenes at school and he was punished less often. He stopped hitting people because Hilda and Eric taught him to ask for permission to leave the room quietly if he felt like that. One day the headmaster called Eric in to see the damage Mickey had done to his electric fire. There had been an argument and Mickey had kicked the fire and now he was once more suspended from school. Eric was furious. He could not believe that the school did not share his pleasure at Mickey's progress which was obvious for all to see; 'Well,' said Eric, 'he only kicked the fire and that's better than kicking the Head.'

It seems unfair that parents like Hilda and Eric who offer love and security to a child like Mickey when all others have passed him by as too old or too difficult, also have to fight for him at every turn. But if fighting equals commitment we have not had greater proof of it.

There are some easier ways for parents and children to claim each other. Danny, the fifteen-year-old, worked alongside his father when they installed a whole new central heating system in their house so that it quickly became Danny's house and Danny's Dad could tell everyone, 'My son and I did it together.'

Sandra's mother let her be claimed by the other children in her large family. Sandra was given special responsibility for one of the little ones and so she became one of the big ones.

Dawn needed to learn by heart the contents of each cupboard, each box, each drawer and each room, in her new home. She is a careful child and, unlike Thelma, she never left a thing out of place. Her parents would come across her, sitting quietly with an improbable collection of things from a rarely used storage shelf, as though she were trying to inhale the life that had produced them. Or sorting and resorting the best china as though she were trying to familiarise herself with every mark on every cup and saucer. Or going through her parents' wardrobe as though she were trying to get to know them through the clothes they wore. Home grown children who take their surroundings for granted would think it strange that Dawn had to spend weeks marking her family through their belongings.

Similarly parents mark their new children through the things they buy for them. No matter how beautifully fitted out a child may be by caretakers and social workers, adopters will want to dress their child in the family image. We have never come across parents who are satisfied with the clothes their children bring with them and we have learnt not to expect them to be. If Mum wears jeans around the place she will not be at all impressed by her new daughter's frilly summer dresses and if Dad wears suits and a tie he will want something more formal than jeans for his teenage son. We ask caretakers not to buy clothes for children moving to families and we ask local authorities to give handsome clothing grants to adopters instead. The first shopping expedition new families make together can be an important step towards commitment.

Josephine's parents felt she was really theirs when she was dressed from top to toe in the new clothes they had bought for her. Every time they took her out of the Children's Home during introductions they put her into the new clothes and she became theirs. Of course children should not be made to feel that their old belongings are awful and have to be discarded. Their favourite sweater and skin tight jeans and ragged anorak should be treasured for their sake, but on the whole children enjoy the fun of choosing new clothes and they do very much want to look like everyone else in the family.

When Keith got his new school uniform he showed it to every visitor. I was given a presentation of grey flannels and white shorts, of grey socks and white shirts, of blazer, cap and tie. The shirts, folded and done up in cellophane, held a special fascination for Keith and he took one out of the wrappings and undid the pins holding it together and shook it out. Then he wanted to put it back just as it was and I offered to help. He looked dubious for a moment but then with great conviction and self satisfaction he said, 'No, it's all right, I'll ask my Mum to do it, she knows about shirts.'

Nick's mother knew about parrots. Nick had taken it into his head that his new parents would buy him a talking bird, but they could not have a bird in the house because they already had two cats who also liked birds and Nick accepted that. Nick looked forward to coming to live in his new house. He liked the big room he had helped to get ready for himself and many of his own things were already waiting for him. When he came for good and went upstairs, it said 'Nick's Room' on his door. He had not expected that. When he went in there was a life-sized silk and woollen parrot sitting on a perch over his bed which had a new duvet and new pillows covered in bright parrot colours. Nick had not known before that bedclothes could be bought for people rather than for boarding schools or Children's Homes. The parrot could not talk, but it said all that needed to be said to Nick about the place that was prepared for him.

Guy's parents thought they knew about footballs. They knew that because Guy had a physical disability, sport was a challenge for him. They agreed when he was nine that he could have a real football if he saved some of his own pocket money towards it. He saved and saved and talked of little else. Then came the great Saturday morning when Dad took Guy out to buy it. But when they got to the sports shop Guy became less enthusiastic and then changed his mind altogether. He said he would rather have a fancy lunch box, like all the other boys in his class. So they bought a lunch box and the football has not been heard of since. Ultimately commitment means letting your adopted child be free and a person in his own right, even if that means he wants to be like everybody else.

The final and official commitment is legal adoption, when children in every sense except the biological one become the children of the parent or parents who adopt them. Families which seem to have shaken down together long before the court hearing have told us that the adoption itself has still been a relief and a reward, like a seal of approval, or a milestone passed or just a celebration of their commitment to each other. Children who have been moved many times and for many reasons, may not be able to make that final commitment themselves until they are adopted. Some children demonstrate every kind of behaviour problem up to the adoption and seem only then to relax and to believe that nothing they can do will get them sent back. Other children do not seem able to behave naturally until after they are adopted in case they are sent back before they belong.

Sandra is a well groomed courteous teenager now. She sings in the school choir, learns the piano and is a reliable family member. Her adoption is under way but is taking longer than she expected and she is showing flashes of her old anger. She needs that final proof that she is acceptable and any delay means uncertainty. Selwyn, in the same family, ransacked his mother's room the day before the adoption hearing was due, just to make sure she really meant to have him whatever he did. Mickey was desperate to be adopted and when the Judge asked him whether he knew his real mother he said reprovingly, 'She's my real mother,' and pointed at Hilda who was about to become his parent. 'The other one only had me,' he explained.

Ivor could not wait to get back to the house after the hearing and his single father did not know why. Ivor opened the door and stood still. 'Hello, Home' he said. But not all children are over-awed or even impressed by the occasion of their adoption. Diane, the four-year-old Down's syndrome child, would not sit still or be quiet while the Judge talked to her parents and finally began to screech. The Judge, hoping to pacify her gave her his large bunch of keys, and Diane, with an unerring aim, threw them back at his face. The parents were not amused, but the Judge made the order.

Judges have been intrigued by some of the families we have presented, but only once has a Judge suggested that the parents might be taking on too much and that they should wait another year before finalising the adoption. They waited a year and their blind Down's syndrome baby is now adopted.

Six of our families have preferred to make a permanent commitment without a legal blessing because they have taken multiply handicapped children who seem not to understand the difference and these parents say that they feel more sure of securing the best for their disabled child in the future if the full weight of a local authority is behind them. Yet most parents say exactly the opposite and do not feel safe to plan the future until an adoption order is made. We are most happy when each child is adopted, but we cannot say that adoptive placements are working better than the other permanent arrangements we have made.

Legal adoption will not remove every problem and may not remove any at all. Children who are not and cannot be adopted will also find security with substitute parents. But adoption remains the only way, apart from birth, of becoming a family both socially and legally with all that implies about independence, autonomy and responsibility. 'Don't forget to find me a family,' Geoffrey called after Hilary each time she left the nursery where he still lived when he was seven. When he got his family, he and his parents worked hard to claim each other. Geoffrey was a little boy who needed operations and the experience of hospitals and pain bonded them together. When I went to see him after his adoption I asked him what he had been doing and he said: 'Just watching trains, it's nice watching trains with your family.'

13 Clients, Colleagues or Friends? – The Adoption Service

Our families are not clients, of that they and we are quite sure. At least, not clients in the social work sense of people who request or require some kind of intervention to help them function. Nor are they clients buying representation and giving instructions as they would be if they went to consult a solicitor or an architect, for we do *not* provide children for parents; it is always the other way round. If anyone is a client, it is the child. We take our instructions from the local authority in whose care the child is and we act for the child who needs parents by finding some. Geoffrey was right to remind us and himself that our job is to find him parents. He enjoyed his chats with Hilary about his life in the nursery, and he was interested in families, and he was enthusiastic about making a poster and his own history book, but he also wanted to make sure that we had our instructions straight.

In social work, and adoption is social work and we are social workers, it is often said that adopters and foster parents are not clients because they are colleagues. We certainly want to work alongside our families, but should they become colleagues? I do not want to become my midwife's colleague. I want to consult her freely about having a child, but do not expect her to consult me about another patient. I do not want her to act in a superior way or to confuse me with her jargon or to mystify me with her expertise, but I do want to feel that she is paid to do something I am not and that she can do it. I also want her to acknowledge me as a person who is not only becoming a mother but who may have other skills in other areas. I do want to have all the available up-to-date information about childbirth, to be included in the plans for my pregnancy and delivery, and to have a say about how my baby

109

will be born. If I want to squat then it is the midwife's job to make sure that that is the way it will be, but I should like her to retain the responsibility for the baby's safe birth. I expect my midwife to be available at the crucial times and do not think I should be required to start labour in her working hours, whatever some hospitals may try to advocate. But I expect her to make demands on me too. As an active partner in the enterprise I should want my midwife to know that I am capable of a great deal of effort and self discipline. I do not think that I owe it to her to have a problem-free delivery though I should like to be able to rely on her to make it as painless as possible. Finally, if something goes wrong I do want her to treat me as an equal, but I would not like her to think that because I am an equal I do not need explanations and counselling and comfort. We also have a responsibility to see parents through their preparation for adoption and introductions to their new child. If they are not getting what they need we should expect them to feel free to say so. And families should also expect us to review and renew our skills so that they can use our experience and resources to further their own plans to build a family.

It is dangerous to be lulled into the comfortable position of making families into colleagues. Seductive to imagine that they and we are doing the same thing and to forget that they are having a child and we are doing a job. They may be far more expert than we are, but that makes them into expert parents not into colleagues. It can be a relief to share our own working problems with sympathetic parents at the end of a long day, much easier than concentrating on the problems in the adoptive family, especially if the family is being very accommodating and not forcing the problems to our attention. This happened with Ben's family when they took a second child.

The child, an older Down's syndrome girl, was not settling but they couldn't bear to tell me how very bad things were because it was a lean time for Parents for Children just then and they knew all about it as they had become extended colleagues. They knew that one adoptive single mother was ill and that a child was lying paralysed in hospital and that most of the Parents for Children team were across the

Atlantic contributing to an international conference. So the family suffered in silence while they supported me and the placement disrupted. It would probably have disrupted anyway but the parents had a right to something more geared to their personal needs than an exchange with a colleague. They were both people who had plenty of colleagues to consult, but there was no other adoption worker available who had any knowledge of the child, the adoptive family to date, and the particular problems of second placements.

If not colleagues, then perhaps the families who adopt through Parents for Children become our friends? We get to know each other and we do not keep our distance. We spend many hours together and share some deep feelings. If we travel by train, we are met at the station and we eat together and parents have said to us, 'You're not like a social worker you're more like a friend.' Or they have explained our visits to their children in this way: 'She comes because she is a friend of the family.' I hope we are friendly and we do feel friendly towards every one of our families but we are certainly social workers. People come to see us because they want to build a family; we see families because that is our job and we are well paid for it. The fact that it is a job we have chosen, a job that we like and that we do not feel compelled to count all the hours we work is our good fortune.

We learn a great deal about families and they learn something about us when we work with them but it all relates to adopting a child. It may be appropriate to share with parents our own experience of a rebellious teenager, if it is relevant to their experience with their child now, but it would hardly be appropriate to tell them of a daughter's latest escapade or a nephew's examination results just to keep them well informed. Whereas they will rightly want to talk about every aspect of their child's progress.

We do not on the whole discuss the latest film together, what we did last night, political opinion, travel, mutual acquaintances, job opportunities or when to move house and all the other many things which are discussed by friends. A change of job or a holiday or a move may affect the adoption and the family may want to talk to us about the problems they foresee. However, although the majority of families have changed jobs or moved house while we have worked with them, not one has asked us to help them reach a decision. That is what friends are for and the rest of the family. Friends are also for doing things with. For sharing holidays, for exchanging leisurely visits, for going to the pictures and for looking after each other's children. We do none of these things.

What is left if people who work closely together are not each other clients, must not become colleagues and are not friends? We are content to be friendly social workers who specialise in adoption and we hope that our families are content to be the consumers of a friendly specialist service. Like all consumers, they have a right to know what that service is.

We offer to prepare families for adoption and to give them every possible opportunity to learn everything there is about the child they want. It is our responsibility to make them understand, as far as we can understand it ourselves, what taking on this child will mean for them. We are not doing our job if we know that a child will never walk, but let the parents think she will if she is loved enough. Of course we cannot and would not wish to stop people having their secret hopes and fantasies – we all believe that our ugly ducklings would be swans if only the prince would come – but there is a difference between having an inner resistance to hopelessness and not hearing what is said because the meaning is not acceptable. We would be giving a very bad service if we encouraged Fay's parents to think that she will become independent in time or if we let Dawn's parents think that time will heal all. We need to convey exactly what it means that twelve-year-old Marion cannot go to the shops on her own or that Josephine's fluid level has to be checked night and day for survival.

We continue our service by taking on the overall management of introductions and placement – the trickiest phase of adoption and the only one we conduct, or rather, orchestrate. It is the delivery, and, although only the parent and the child will know how it feels, the midwife can hear the heartbeat, gauge the oxygen and measure the readiness. A push at the wrong moment can cause a tear, and unnecessary delay can cause damage. A rhythmic and sensitive working together will produce the best placement.

The bulk of the service to families is post placement support. I asked one of our single parents who has adopted two multiply handicapped children and who has had to lean heavily on our support, what she would advise social workers to do to improve this part of the service. 'Oh just hang about,' she said We have to hang about to understand what each family requires of us because it is always different and there is not much point in offering the most efficient and streamlined service if it is not what the consumer wants. It is no good insisting that a service is supportive if it does not support the consumer and only the family can tell us what is supportive and what is not.

Most car owners will have their car regularly serviced for the sake of the car and their peace of mind. They will want the garage to provide an expert who will not waste their time and money, which tinkering friends and colleagues are rather apt to do. They will want to have an explanation of why the car is behaving in a peculiar way but they will not be prepared to become mechanics in order to understand the explanation. If there is something potentially dangerous they would like to hear about it in good time. They would not thank the mechanic if the big end dropped off and he had not alerted them because he had not wanted to upset them. On the other hand, it is their car and they are unlikely to thank the mechanic either, for telling them how to drive it when they have been driving for years, how fast to go – they can read the road signs – or where to travel. If they ask for advice, the mechanic will probably be able to give it because he has seen a lot of cars. While the car is under guarantee the garage may even remind the owners of the service they should have and make the required appointment well in advance, but once the car is out of guarantee they are on their own and have to rely on their instincts and knowledge and the availability of their friendly mechanic to keep the car on the road. And they ought not to have to rely too much on that one particular mechanic, because if it is a good garage it will have other equally competent workers who will know their car. Children are not cars and adopters are not giving birth any more than we are midwives, let alone mechanics, but the principles of an expert consumer service hold well enough for an adoption agency.

The post placement service before legal adoption has to meet the regulations laid down by the Department of Health and Social Security and the courts according to the age of the child and the duration of the placement. We try to merge these statutory requirements with adopters' needs.

Most families like frequent visits early on, becoming gradually more spaced out, and they want us to be flexible enough to respond to a changing situation. Jenny's parents, the Deightons, accepted her slow progress even when it came to a standstill and asked for only token support when the adoption was delayed. They liked to know we were there, they said. But when Jenny suddenly, after two good years, exploded into lies and bedwetting and stealing they wanted help fast and they could ask for it because the service was there for the asking. We juggled with our diaries and freed a whole day immediately to give an emergency service. Jenny regained her former equilibrium after the adoption and the parents regained their confidence, but it took that whole day of taking stock together to get over the hump.

Marion's mother said that the most helpful support for her was knowing that we would ring every Wednesday, then later every other Wednesday and for a long time after that the first Wednesday of every month. She said she knew no matter what happened she would be able to talk about every little thing that bothered her and had been building up. This was a long distance family who might have had a better service from a neighbourhood agency, but as we placed the child we had to make the most of the telephone between our monthly visits.

Brenda, who worked on her own no matter what was on offer, always made it clear that she would accept the minimum service only and even then each statutory visit seemed like an imposition. She rightly did not consider herself our client, friend or colleague but she did not seem keen on consuming our service either. That seems fair enough in retrospect, but at the time, those monthly visits to the further end of Suffolk, dragging on for two years because of the delayed adoption, became the low point of my working life. The family and the agency lost confidence in one another and it cannot surely, be supportive to have to go on using a service you do not choose to have; just as it is very dispiriting to go on giving a service that is not put to use. However, when it came to the adoption hearing, this same parent and all her family gave me a particularly warm and considerate welcome and Brenda has conveyed publicly that she is a satisfied consumer of a responsive service. We are still trying to learn from that.

The service, whatever it achieves or fails to provide, is given with the aim of transferring power from the local authorities, the social workers, the adoption agency and all the parts of the corporate parent, to the only people who are going to matter, the adopters. Parents who have already been handed the responsibility of looking after the new child also need to feel that they have the authority to act on behalf of their child when they come face to face with the education system, the medical profession, the social services, grandparents, neighbours and friends. They must be allowed to let the child use their family name as soon as he is ready – and James couldn't wait to put his new name on his library tickets and school register. Another boy, who was too old to be adopted, asked for his name to be changed by deed poll.

We must make sure that all official letters are addressed to the parents correctly and not to some mythical Mr and Mrs Brown because Brown is the name by which the child has been known. We must make sure that people who have known the child as Brown do not go on sending birthday cards to John Brown when he has become John Smith. And we must make sure that John Smith is not singled out from the rest of his family at Christmas by a social worker who is still sending presents to a child in care.

It is no good pretending to ourselves or the family that their child does not remain in care until an adoption order is made, but there are ways of transferring power in the meantime. Authorisation for medical treatment can be delegated to prospective adopters so that never again will a mother be left helpless by her son's bedside in hospital, unqualified to sign the paper that will enable him to have a necessary, but not an urgent operation. Geoffrey had to have cosmetic surgery on both eyes and the local authority obtained permission from his natural parents because he was not yet legally adopted. The surgeon decided to do one eye at a time and sent Geoffrey home for a month's rest in between. Geoffrey was ready for the second operation, in his white gown with his long woolly white socks on and in a drowsy state after his premedication, when the medical team realised that as this was a second operation, a second consent form would have to be signed. And his adoptive mother, who had stayed with him day and night during his first hospitalisation and was preparing to stay for this one, was not able to sign that paper. She had to take Geoffrey home and two weeks later with the form duly completed by the original parents who have not seen Geoffrey since he was a baby, they had to return to the hospital and Geoffrey had to 'be a brave little boy' all over again. Many people, including the original parents, were unnecessarily distressed. If parents who give birth to a child also give their consent to adoption it does not seem sensitive or compassionate to insist that they retain responsibility for medical treatment until the last possible moment. Neither is it sensitive or compassionate to ask adopters to be parents with exception clauses.

Nor must we fall into the trap of thinking that adopters need a go-between. We cannot talk to teachers or the education officer or the psychologist or the health visitor about the new child in the family as well as the parents can, although we would want to support families in any negotiations if they wanted our help. It is a simple rule we try to follow; if a family is good enough to become the child's family, then it is good enough to take over the rights and duties of parents.

The post placement service itself is an acknowledgement of the new family. We do not take the children out for treats when we visit, but we do try to provide a kind of expert sounding board and mirror for all the family. Neighbours, friends and relatives also perform this service for each other but, however willing, they have not experienced bringing up a child like Keith or Sandra or James and are unlikely to have adopted a disabled child. Often well meaning friends will assure adopters that their new child is behaving quite normally for his age when he is clearly not. Concerned relatives may insist that the child will not always be handicapped when she surely will be. We can monitor what is happening for the parents who are too close to the action to notice the changes we see. Hannah seemed to melt and soften month by month, Josephine was transformed from a limp, withdrawn baby to a toddler glowing with health and a zest for life, Mickey changed from an unmanageable youth to an engaging young man and by describing what we could see we confirmed it for the parents. This does not immediately make Hannah or Josephine or Mickey like other ordinary children, but generally there is progress and it can be measured. When there is not and when the initial excitement of achievement gives way to the daily chores of child care, then a sounding board can become even more necessary. Someone who will listen to complaints, ideas, theories and participate in possible solutions. Someone who has a vested interest in making the placement work and who should be prepared to be critical and honest. Someone who bears some responsibility for allowing the placement to disrupt, if that is what must finally happen. Someone who can detect a glimmer of hope in a depressing situation or notice the danger signals when the family is blithely enjoying a honeymoon period. When Keith was ill and unreasonable and his mother could do no more, she needed to know how closely the illness had bonded them together; and when Nick seemed to be losing all contact with his natural family his new parents had to know that he could not bring up his past unless they did.

But families need more than mirrors and sounding boards. They need reliable information at all times. They may need to know about welfare rights, housing and support groups. They will need some guidance through the adoption procedure, especially if it is a complicated case that could rebound on their child. Nick's parents talk to him often now about his birth family and they have been able to explain to him that his original mother and father feel very mixed up about his adoption. They want him to have a family of his own, but they feel so badly about their inability to be his parents that they find it difficult to sign the consent forms for the adoption.

Post adoption, the service is entirely a matter between the parents and the agency. At Parents for Children we make a plan with each family soon after the adoption hearing. The post adoption service is available until the child is eighteen, but we have found that some families, especially single parents with handicapped children, want to stay in contact longer, because their children need more. John and his son Harry who is now a grown-up young man, come regularly to our office to send out the three hundred odd newsheets to the people on our mailing list. This provides Harry with the kind of work Down's syndrome people can do and it gives John a chance both to help out and to chat to the Parents for Children workers about 'Life with Harry'. Some parents want to continue after the adoption with lengthy home visits once a month, fixed well ahead of time. Others are glad to be on their own and would rather know that they can telephone us if they want us, or ask us to telephone them. Most families want something in between, at regular intervals.

We want to keep in touch with families, too, because that is the way we learn what works and what does not and we ask whether we may visit at least once a year even if the family has become completely self-supporting. We have been grateful to families who take this part of the work as seriously as adoption itself. They regard it as their responsibility to feed back information to us and we regard their contribution as central to the agency's development. We learn little if we know that the three children have settled on the farm and been adopted, but we can try to learn from the progress of three young black city children growing up with white parents on a remote farm in Norfolk. We can learn how much their first, deprived years have a bearing on their schooling now. We can learn about one family's attempt at multiracial, multicultural living, and we can learn endlessly from parents who are finding original and creative ways of bringing up three children who desperately, each of them, cry out for the individual attention they never had.

When they arrived, Belinda, Tony and Norman watched each other like little hawks to see who was getting more of what. Bread, apples or cuddles, it was all the same, they could not tolerate having less. When grandmother called, all three of them hurled themselves at her at exactly the same time so that her chair toppled over and Grandma had to be rescued from the kitchen floor. Meal times were torture for the adults. The children outdid each other in eating and shouting. They were the nearest human things to wild tornados. We fondly imagine that brothers and sisters brought up in care will be fiercely loyal to each other. We forget that they are more likely to fight each other for the little they have to share between them. These parents could not and did not tackle everything at once. First they devised ways of giving each child appropriate and individual attention. Dad took Norman to clean out the pigs while Grandpa showed Tony how to tether the goats, and Belinda learned to knead the dough and bake the bread and so on until each child would become absorbed in a task and assured that there was enough of everything to go round.

If we had not kept in touch with this family long after they needed us and after the children were adopted, we would not have seen how Belinda breeds rabbits, how Norman has become quite a goatherd, and how Tony runs a small chicken business. He could not quite get the point of maths at school, so his parents have encouraged him to buy the chicks and rear them, to buy the chicken food and make the chicken run and to sell the eggs back to his mother. He is doing very well and his book keeping shows that he is making a profit.

Meal times with this family are a pleasure now. The children are not greedy and show consideration, not only for their parents and their visitors, but for each other. They make sure that everyone else has enough before they do, and that everyone has a chance to speak. This has not been achieved by love alone or overnight. It took more than two years of patient daily teaching and example. Always one thing at a time. The parents tackled the 'shouting each other down' by making one firm rule. The children had to take it in strict turns to speak at the table and they had to leave the table if they disobeyed. They discovered it was more fun than all talking at once because this way their mother and father could hear what they said and in time they even began to listen to each other.

Families not only contribute by allowing us to go on visiting after adoption, but also more directly by helping us to teach other social workers and prepare other parents. Whenever we have included adopters in a teaching programme it has made more impact than if we have recounted what adopters have said or done. Prospective adopters always say that meeting adoptive parents was the most valuable part of their preparation. So we work side by side with our families from the beginning and there is not necessarily an end. As adoption workers we cannot ask for more than to work side by side, not with clients, friends or colleagues, but with adopters.

14 The Beauty Spot – Handicapped Children

'Why would someone do such an extraordinary thing?' 'What makes people want to adopt a severely disabled child?' 'How can anyone choose to have a retarded teenager?' 'Isn't there something wrong with families which deliberately become handicapped?' We are asked these questions over and over again. We do not wholly understand the answers we give, but we can say that there are people who begin by wanting to adopt an ordinary child and adopt a disabled child because they respond to the need. That there are parents who consider retardation a blessing and that there are families which thrive on the challenge of being labelled handicapped. The stories of some of these families may provide better answers.

Bridgid and Joe claimed each other in a very special way. Bridgid was adopted in Ireland thirty years ago. She must have been an exceptionally bright and pretty child, for she is certainly an exceptionally intelligent and attractive woman. Her adoptive parents were an unhappy couple whose two handicapped daughters had died as infants. The mother's mind became unbalanced and the father was drunk when he was home. Bridgid was abused and made to feel that it was her fault that her sisters were dead. She had to kneel by their graves and ask for forgiveness every Sunday. When she was ten the authorities became concerned about her and she was taken into care and placed in a large orphanage. She stayed there until she was eighteen and while she was there she became mute; she just stopped speaking. She remembers very well her hatred of the authority which was supposed to protect her from the parents she feared, but also loved.

Now Bridgid no longer had to go to the cemetery on Sunday but on Sunday the orphanage doors were opened to couples in search of a child. The children were dressed up in frills and flounces and starched white shirts and they stood in rows to receive the visitors. Bridgid watched and scowled while the liveliest, most perfect babies were picked up and cooed over and the dull, disabled and disfigured ones were left behind, together with most of the older children who were in any case only considered as possible cheap labour for large families. Bridgid made quite sure that no one would ever choose her.

As she grew up, silent and stony faced, she relented only to the babies and children who were constantly being left behind. She did not co-operate at school where she was known as one of the 'Home's Children' and separated from respectable children living with their families. She learned to fight for herself and became an expert at joining the same sweet queue twice in the orphanage on Saturdays. She was not a particularly likeable girl, but some of the nuns at the orphanage understood her sympathy for the disadvantaged and encouraged her to train as a nurse for mentally handicapped people.

Bridgid came to England and began to speak again. She educated herself and passed her examinations to become a nurse. She was often depressed and sometimes went wild on motorbikes; no more so than many young adults but unlike others of her age she was alone and responsible to no one. Until she met people like herself, who chose to work and live with mentally handicapped children and who also chose to look after her. Bridgid has become part of a strong and mutually supportive network of carers. There is a kind of freemasonry among people concerned with handicap; an understanding and compassion for each other as well as their disabled charges. They are 'into handicap' like one could be 'into meditation' or 'into leading the good life'.

There are many associations for handicapped people, there are parent groups, support groups and pressure groups. There are educational projects, residential projects and social clubs and most of them know of each other and are inter-connected. This may sound as though there is more than adequate and very appropriate provision for all disabled people. There is not, but it is due to Bridgid and her friends who may be parents, priests, volunteers, nurses, doctors, social workers, influential writers or politicians, that there is any provision in the community at all. And there are still vast institutions outside our major cities where disabled people who are not gathered up by the network linger as children and vegetate as adults.

Bridgid worked in one such institution and it confirmed her belief that subnormality hospitals are not homes for children. She was a little more comfortable working in a special Home for severely retarded children but not for long. She heard of Parents for Children, understood that single parents could adopt, and decided she would give everything to one or two children rather than a very little to many.

Bridgid came to see us on one of her days off from the special Children's Home. She was so nervous that she trembled but she was resolute. She said, 'I want to adopt the most handicapped child you have.' Just sometimes it happens that someone walks in for the first time and you know it is going to work. Not smoothly, not without friction or hold ups, but it was going to work and we knew it and were astounded because she was the parent we had been looking for: single, a nurse, 'into handicap' and with experience of problems overcome; the parent for Joe we thought we would never find.

We had set out to prove that every child is adoptable but we feared we had gone too far in taking on Joe. We were not at all sure what we could offer him and whether he had anything to offer a family. He was six years old and suffered from a rare degenerative and fatal disease. We knew and any prospective parents would have to know, that Joe would die in childhood. Tuberous sclerosis affected his brain and all his organs. He was severely retarded, epileptic, only partially sighted, hardly able to walk and never likely to speak. He lived in a world of his own, making bizarre sounds and movements, seemingly unable to make contact with another human being. In his Children's Home he had to be barricaded off from the other children because he was violent and uncontrollable. He ate with his hands, could not dress himself or keep himself clean and he had to wear nappies. There were tales of a bookcase overturned, a radiator pulled off a wall and every toy in sight smashed to pieces, but Joe could also be docile. He spent many waking hours plucking and pinging a piece of red toy

railway track accompanied by a whole range of noises signi-
fying delight.

Bridgid looked at Joe's poster and said, yes, he was the child
for her, he even looked like her she noted, and Joe, for many
reasons, was the name most close to her heart. Then she gave
us all the reasons why we might not accept her. Her own
background would be against her she thought, her history of
depression and instability would not help. She had little
money and lived in a furnished room. If she gave up work she
would have to live on social security benefits. She had no
family to support her. She had nothing to offer, she said,
except an untried ability to be a parent, a hunger to love a
handicapped child and a determination to improve the quality
of Joe's life; and she would fight us for him. She did not have
to, but we had to fight by her side to convince the caretakers,
the administrators and the social workers that Bridgid should
have Joe.

Doctors gave the opinion that Joe needed nursing not
parenting, but we were encouraged by our own medical
adviser's contrary view. His houseparents could not but be
suspicious of a single woman who was proposing to share her
life with a child they could not contain, and the social workers
who had referred him had not expected us to find a family and
now mistrusted our choice. They thought it perverse of a
woman who had succeeded in spite of everything, as Bridgid
had, to throw it all away, as they saw it, to live on a pittance
in order to adopt a dying child. They tried to dissuade her
altogether. They could not agree with our judgement that
only a single parent could manage Joe because he would
disrupt any partnership. They tried to persuade Bridgid to
foster Joe and they would pay well. And when Bridgid insisted
on adoption they insisted on a year's waiting period. So
Bridgid became Joe's mother, she reared him, loved him and
nursed him, but she was not allowed to adopt him for twelve
months. It is greatly to their credit and must be recorded, that
the workers from that local authority who saw the placement
through, changed their minds generously, persuaded by
Bridgid and Joe that in spite of on-going problems and frequent conflict, this was an adoption to be prized.

Bridgid and Joe learned to love life together. Joe had hardly ever been out of the grounds of the Children's Home and he was fascinated by the noises of the street, the bustle in the shops, the sounds of rustling leaves and running water and the gurgling of drains. He became obsessed with drains and during her visits to the Children's Home, while she was getting to know Joe, Bridgid spent many hours with him sitting by the side of the road listening to drains. She meant to start from exactly where he was. And during introductions she began to take Joe on buses and trains as they would not have a car. She introduced him to her friends and their homes for they would not live in seclusion, and she bought him bright new clothes for he was a beautiful child and she would make him 'look like a prince'. Bridgid had a demanding job but she managed to see Joe once a week and every weekend until he seemed ready to come and live with her. No one could be sure he was ready, his behaviour in the Home was as odd as it had ever been, but Bridgid saw that he knew her and that he relaxed when he was with her.

Bridgid also had to make herself ready. She needed somewhere to live, she needed to eke out the supplementary benefit she would claim with attendance and mobility allowances for Joe and she had to establish her rights to services as the single mother-to-be of a disabled child. She had to mobilise her supportive network into action because she knew from the beginning that she would have to have regular help and relief. She needed to line up a sympathetic GP who would know something about Joe's disease, a co-operative Health Centre which would provide her with a nappy service and an inventive occupational therapist who would fix aids and adaptations around the flat to give Joe freedom and keep him safe.

Bridgid did it all but not without causing some consternation and giving some offence because she would not hesitate to ask several people, organisations or agencies for the same thing at the same time if that was likely to get the required results more quickly. Or she would confuse us all by agreeing to go one way with one person and then moving off in the opposite direction with another. Or there were times when she could not accept what was being offered by one of the many caring friends and workers around her and then whoever it was would be regarded as useless and hostile, but only for a time. And this set the pattern for all the years to come; not an easy working relationship, but unusually rewarding as well as demanding.

Lastly, Bridgid had to furnish her new home to suit Joe's needs and her own. She achieved something remarkable. The sitting room was the centre and the centre was divided into two. One half was a cosy place with armchairs and a sofa and low tables and soft carpet, pictures and books, flowers and records. The other half of the room was a playground: tough lino on the floor, a sand tray in one corner and a paddling pool in the other; mobiles hanging down from the ceiling, bright posters on the walls and a disco light rotating, throwing light and shade and colour with the press of a button. There was a box with a carefully chosen assortment of toys: red plastic hammers that rang a bell, a great red cuddly Father Christmas, and things that rattled and squeaked, things that caught the light and shone. Somewhere in the box were pieces of red train track and they stayed there for most of the time because Joe had other things to do but he never quite gave them up.

The delicate flower arrangements, and ornaments on the low tables in the grown up half of the room were curiously explored, but never disturbed or broken. The books were handled, but not torn and the records were handed to Bridgid to make music, for music became the greatest pleasure in Joe's life. On his eighth birthday Bridgid bought him a small electric organ so that he could make his own music. This wild child, this boy who we said would not be able to relate, sank into the warmth and colour and gentleness of his new life and left the frustrations of his old life behind him, almost as though they had never been. And he learned to laugh.

The rest of the house was as skilfully arranged around Bridgid and Joe. There were rails along the stairs and passages and within weeks Joe could enjoy the run of the house. No door was closed to him, every room was made safe for him: a guard around the cooker, concealed central heating, cupboards within his reach containing all the things he liked best to eat and a low bed he could safely fall out of but never did. Bathing aids, a raised toilet seat, an electric toothbrush, toothpaste that smelled of strawberries, bubbles in the water and bubbles to blow, made him want to be clean and after a year he was out of nappies and climbing into the bath on his own and wanting to brush his teeth.

The garden was Joe's special place too. There was a fence all round the house with a child proof gate. He could get in and out of the flat as he chose and Bridgid could see him wherever he was. She bought him a swing and he delighted in his new found skill of making himself go higher and higher until visitors flinched, but not Bridgid. When he was not on his swing he liked to touch the grass or to sit at the front of the house and hear the cars go by. Later he got a bicycle and Bridgid taught him to ride it. He wore a crash helmet, the bike had stabilisers and she always walked behind him, but he could ride. Joe who could hardly walk when he came, could run and ride a bike and swing high.

Bridgid and Joe explored the world together. Because she would need two hands to look after him, Bridgid took to carrying a rucksack rather than a handbag and Joe did the same. They made an appealing pair walking down the street, both dressed in red, hand in hand with packs on their backs. They went to concerts and Joe sat quite still and listened. They went to the country and Bridgid shared Joe's pleasure in the feels and smells and sounds and the red flowers. Sometimes they just went and stood for an hour or two on Westminster Bridge. They ate in restaurants because Joe had learnt to use a spoon and they joined other families with disabled children on religious retreats. Joe went to a special school but Bridgid could not agree with the teachers that education was of the greatest importance to him; and she was giving him all the social training he needed. So she kept him home whenever he was tired or there was something to do together.

One Easter they went to Lourdes and Joe was equally excited by the aeroplane and the myriads of candles in the holy grotto. They spent one holiday on a barge on the canals. They regularly had tea with an imposing prelate of the Church. They spent weekends with various members of their network. They enjoyed the present and would not be overwhelmed by the future. Bridgid had felt herself disabled and took on the most disabled child, but together they were not handicapped.

Yet even the present was not always enjoyable.

Occasionally Brigid was exhausted and had to rely on her friends to come in and take over. One winter she was quite seriously ill and Joe had to go and stay with her friends. In spite of all his progress Joe remained a sick child and sometimes he was very sick. The frequency and violence of his fits increased and there were more and more consultations with doctors and periods in hospital. Bridgid was beset by doubts about her own capabilities. She was perplexed by the force of her maternal feelings. She was tormented, not by any fears of disability, disease or even death, but by the fear that she could not be a real mother because she had not had one herself. As Joe became more dependent again, she tried to distance herself from the pain by being the nurse not the mother, but she accepted motherhood long before the end and suffered and mourned when it came, as only parents can.

Bridgid fought everyone those last few months when Joe was nearly ten and she knew he was going to die soon. The doctors, amazed by his progress, had prophesied that he could live until he was fifteen. Her friends and supporters tried to reassure her and to disarm her but she was angry with us all for letting Joe die and she was angry with Joe for dying. Joe had still more fits. He developed a pallor, so different from the healthy glow he had developed on his mother's diet of protein and vegetables. He no longer ate the treats he found in the cupboard and he could not manage the stairs. The teachers agreed that Joe should only come to school when he was well enough. Bridgid got him a wheelchair, a pushchair and they moved to another flat with everything on one level.

The new flat was made ready overnight; Bridgid spared herself and those around her nothing in getting the best deal for Joe. The swing was in the garden but hardly used now. Bridgid brought a bed into the sitting room so that Joe could rest in the centre and never feel on the outside. He became incontinent again, he could do none of the things he had learnt except make contact with his eyes. Bridgid could not tolerate his illness now, she railed against it, she became frantic in her effort to save him, she would have shaken him into life if she could.

Joe died at home in his own bed during a seizure. Bridgid was holding him when he died because he was always scared by his fits and she held him whenever she was near enough. And she tried to resuscitate him.

Three priests officiated at Joe's funeral, in white vestments, because he was a child and it was Easter again. Two young men played the guitar and sang Joe's favourite songs. There were many people in the church: the priests, the young men and all the people who had known and cared for Joe. Like Bridgid, they had only known him for three years, but they said that he had given more than he took away with him now. And they said that the three years of mothering Bridgid had offered him could not be weighed in the balance of joy and grief because they were a priceless gift.

Every time we place a child with a family we wonder what we have done. Not only, will it work, but what will it do to the family and will it be worthwhile for the child? Will the end justify the risks? When we place a child as damaged as Joe we cannot feel confident that he will benefit enough to outweigh the sorrow he will cause his parents. We can only guess that there will be gladness too. We also cannot put Joe and Bridgid's few years together in the balance against Joe's empty years before and the emptiness that followed for Bridgid.

After Joe died I asked Bridgid how I could learn to tell whether people who wanted to adopt a retarded or disabled child could really manage to do it. 'It all depends', she said, 'on whether they have found the beauty spot.' 'What was Joe's beauty spot?' I asked and she replied without hesitation, 'His speechlessness'.

Bridgid would often say that Joe was 'totally daft' and that she loved him for it not in spite of it. She described how he taught her to listen to what he could not say and how she loved that rich silence. She wrote the words Joe could not speak: 'Love me as I am and watch my different ways of movement because that's how I communicate and listen hard to my squeaky sounds, they are usually a request, and look into my face because my eyes speak. If you watch, listen and look, you will find I can communicate very well. Like any little boy I have my dislikes so, please, although it might make you happy, if I eat all my dinner it might make me very unhappy. I can also get sad and withdrawn like you, but remember, given love and security I will become a happier Joe. My Mummy and I communicate very well. Early in the morning when I think she is asleep I visit the kitchen and help myself to biscuits. You see I am learning new skills.'

Other parents of disabled children have told us that they particularly like the way their Down's syndrome daughter wrinkles her button nose and narrows her slanting eyes when she concentrates or the way their son walks all lopsidedly or the funny way he speaks. There are as many beauty spots as there are disabilities. Some people find them and some people cannot see them. Some people may surprise themselves.

Emily's father had many doubts about his capacity to acknowledge a four-year-old daughter who limped and could not smile. He worried in case he was only adopting her out of a sense of duty or to please his wife and that he would never be a proper father. But he found the beauty spot. Emily's struggle to speak with a paralysed face touched his own experience of teaching himself to read music and play the piano which he now does remarkably well. Emily had to memorise the position of tongue, lips and jaw for each sound and then she had to learn ways of getting them into that position before she could begin to speak and be understood. Her father, as a child, had to memorise melodies and pick them out on a piano and then laboriously relate the sounds to the printed notes before he could begin to make the classical music he loved. Emily speaks fluently now, but her parents know the effort she has to make and her speech remains her beauty spot.

Hugh's parents knew his beauty spot before they knew Hugh. They wanted him because he had a kidney disease and would soon have to have dialysis three times a week. He was waiting for a kidney machine and they wanted to wait with him. Hugh was nearly seventeen, but they could not let him face the prospect of hospital and discomfort and anxiety without a family behind him. Before Hugh came to live with them they had to learn to cope with his disability. When he was with them they went on learning together about the new treatment that, although it would save his life, would cause him more pain to begin with. It was a powerful beauty spot and it cemented an unlikely relationship. The parents who had five other children already, had not been looking for a sick seventeen-year-old son and we thought we had little chance of finding a family for Hugh because we considered that age was his biggest handicap.

Hugh had a hard time getting used to dialysis and he needed his family. His parents had a hard time watching his distress and spending whole days in hospital with him, but they were glad they could be there. Now Hugh is accustomed to the treatment and he and his family are waiting for another kidney machine, only this one will be installed in their home.

Sometimes it takes a change of circumstances for the beauty spot to appear. Gwen and Ray were a young couple with one small, home-grown daughter. They really wanted twelve-year-old Marion who was brain damaged and a slow learner with a sad history, but they found it difficult to relate to her during introductions. Nothing had worked for Marion so far. Her birth mother had been unable to look after her, her foster parents no longer wanted her when she developed a will of her own and her first adoptive parents had separated and left her once more without a family. She was living with friends of this last family and she had grown fond of them, but they were unsettled themselves and could not keep her either. Gwen and Ray understood Marion's great need to belong and they could see why she found it so hard to relax with them, but they did not find her constant bids for attention, her greed and overweight and her disobedience at all endearing. Nevertheless they persevered all through January and February. They travelled long distances to see her. They were marooned with her in snow and ice, and to her great amusement Ray stepped into a snowdrift and almost disappeared from sight.

On the day Marion was to go and live with them Gwen and Ray came to collect her by car as arranged. But by the time they arrived, Marion was in hospital, admitted as an emergency case, suffering from an unidentified illness. She was very ill. She lay still and was only half conscious. Every now and then she would sit up suddenly to be sick. She seemed to be talking nonsense. Gwen and Ray were shocked to see their child in such a plight. She had become their child in that moment. They insisted that she should be formally placed with them there and then, and they would do for her whatever had to be done. Luckily the delegation of medical authority was in the envelope we had prepared for them, together with all the papers and information they would need as parents.

Marion rapidly got worse and her parents stayed with her. Towards the evening she had a major epileptic fit, stopped breathing and had to be revived. Consultants were called and Marion was rushed to another hospital twenty miles away for brain surgery. Gwen went in the ambulance and Ray followed by car. The operation was exploratory and revealed that there was damage to the stem of the brain, but no clue as to the cause. For three days Marion's life was in danger and her parents stayed at her side. Then, as she recovered from the surgery it became apparent that Marion was totally paralysed. She could literally not move a finger or anything else. Tubes went into her body and came out of it. She could not even cough or swallow.

After two weeks she was able to eat a little, to move her lips laboriously and to say a few words. No other improvement was expected. The damage to the stem of the brain was responsible for the paralysis and the damage could not be repaired.

So family life for Gwen and Ray and Marion began with hospital visits, and Ruth came too. Five-year-old Ruth got to know her sister lying motionless in a hospital bed with a shaved and bandaged head, teeth broken during the emergency anaesthetic and a partially chewed away lip. Marion, who had always bitten her nails, was now chewing the only piece of herself she could reach with her teeth. It is one of the wonders of this placement, that Ruth and Marion have developed a deep affection for each other, a tender sisterly concern which must surely have its roots in that depressing hospital room.

Marion stayed in hospital for five months. Twice a week for five months her parents made the trek from the south to the east of England. At weekends they brought Ruth and their caravan and stayed near the hospital grounds. They travelled more than a thousand miles each week to see Marion and they never lost their belief that Marion would get better. Somehow, sometime, they knew she would get better.

It was Ray who first saw Marion move a finger. The doctor and the nurses humoured him. Then Gwen saw it too, hardly a movement, more like a flutter in her limbs. Slowly and pain-fully movement came back. After three months Marion could sit in a chair and feed herself and do simple things with her hands. Gwen and Ray gave her the keys to their house and told her that they were waiting for her to come home. She came in August, walking unsteadily, and the doctors were as mystified by her recovery as they had been by her illness. The only explanation was her terrific will to live. They said that her parents had saved her life.

Marion recovered almost completely, but her return towards normality was not a return to her previous irritating behaviour. She was more quiet, more content, less greedy and in fact she is the child who never asks for anything. She helps both parents because she really likes doing all the chores in the house and the garden. Her lip has been repaired and her teeth have been fixed. She is slim and pretty and nearly grown up now and will be able to work under supervision. There have been problems over the years, but most daughters cause their parents some anxiety.

Gwen and Ray wish that Marion was more ready to make demands, to stand up for herself, to show her feelings, for they know that her desire to please is just another way of dealing with her buried fears and uncertainties. But it is behaviour to which they can respond. Marion may have been changed by her illness, but it was not her personality that changed, only her way of expressing it. Perhaps, once her parents had found her beauty spot – her helplessness and her need for protection – she could trust enough to stop provoking them to send her back. She must have known they never would, as they had brought her back to life.

It is easier for adoptive parents to appreciate their children's disabilities because unlike natural parents they have not had to live through the crisis and shock of the birth, nor do they mourn for the healthy infant they might have had. Josephine's parents saw every one of her handicaps as special gifts. Will they be able to feel the same way about Sheeraz? Both children are blind but do they have the same beauty spots?

Even people like Bridgid cannot find the beauty spot in every child. While Joe was still with her, she tried to introduce two other children into the family. First it was Thelma who

wanted to send Joe away and then it was Len, a Down's
syndrome boy who had terrible rages and did not know when
he was hurting Joe. She could not go on with either, but
even before Joe died her heart went out to Margery, the girl in
the wheelchair, who was as daft in her body, Bridgid said, as
Joe was in his mind. Margery was already a teenager and the
families who came forward for her retreated again when they
understood exactly how disabled she was and how dependent
she would always be. Bridgid could not even think of having
her while Joe was so ill but she did not forget her and even
when she was mourning for Joe she kept an eye on Margery. A
year later Margery was still without parents and Bridgid felt
ready to have the daughter who would not be expected to
replace her son.

    Margery slipped into life with Bridgid. Mother and daugh-
ter share very similar experiences of abuse, abandonment and
death. They have allowed each other to grieve for the families
they have lost while they build a new family together. Margery
will stop chattering and Bridgid recounts with pride all the
amusing things she says. Bridgid has had to learn what it
means to be in a wheelchair. They have had to move house
again to accommodate the range of wheelchairs Margery
needs, to move about indoors, to go out, to go to school. One
she can work herself, one has to be pushed, and one can be
folded. Bridgid found it harder to come to terms with the
wheelchairs than with the disabled child. She has given us a
piece of advice. 'Next time you place a child in a wheelchair
place the wheelchairs first and don't place the child until the
adopters have settled down with the chairs.'

    Bridgid and Margery are still struggling with becoming a
handicapped family because that is what they are. Even so
Margery knows that she is more than a child in a wheelchair.
When she was introduced to a boy of her own age he said to
her: 'You're pretty', and she said, 'I know.' 'How do you
know?' he asked her and she answered, 'Bridgid told me.' It
was also Bridgid who told her: 'I picked the one who couldn't
walk.'

15   Parents are not Enough

Adopters are not wizards. If they seem able to work miracles it is because there is something miraculous about the way a child can change. Children change all the time and very fast. If children have been in care and their development has been delayed, they can astonish us by the way they can catch up when they are adopted. 'Joe has changed beyond all recognition,' the people who knew him before used to tell Bridgid. But Joe had an awful lot of catching up to do and Bridgid, as she liked to remind us, was not a saint or a lunatic or a wizard, but a good enough parent who needed all the support she could get. She could not have managed without her friends, without the right medical and educational services, without suitable housing and an adequate income.

Joe and Bridgid were fortunate because all the help they needed was available, even if Bridgid had to push for some of it. But in other places, for other families, help is not available however hard they might be willing to push. Luke was eleven and profoundly deaf. There was no way he could be educated in an ordinary school and his partially deaf adoptive father knew it. The only school that would ever teach Luke to communicate was a boarding school two and a half hours away by car and inaccessible by public transport.

Both adoptive parents feared that Luke would not comprehend why he was moving from his Children's Home and day school to live in a new school during the week and with two strangers every weekend. They did not feel confident about becoming part-time parents, knowing it would be hard enough for Luke to attach himself to a full-time family, but nevertheless they decided to go ahead. They took enormous risks and five years later they are still risking, but Luke has at last learnt to recognise language and to speak so that he has also learnt to understand his very special situation.

Luke's adoptive parents have persevered against odds which can damage the relationship between natural parents and a deaf child or even make for difficulties between parents and their normal children. As one eleven-year-old girl said to her mother after her first term at boarding school: 'I don't see enough of your face.' Adopted children like Luke have never seen enough of anyone's face and it is asking almost the impossible of families, who need to dig in together, to separate so soon and so much.

Mickey, the boy who showed progress by not kicking the headmaster, still managed to get himself expelled, eventually, from his special school and his parents, who can fight harder than any we know, have had to accept boarding school education for him. They compelled their local education authority to offer Mickey a place in the local comprehensive school but he could not cope with being one among so many. They kept him at home and they wrote to their Member of Parliament; if they had been able to create a school for him they would have done it, because they had not found their fourteen-year-old son in order to send him off to live with strangers. But in the end they had to give in. There was not a school to suit Mickey in the whole county. Mickey needed schooling and he needed to be with other children. Like Luke he needed parents more than anything, but parents were not enough.

Peter's mother, herself a teacher, was in a position to insist that her Down's syndrome son should have the opportunity of normal education for as long as possible. So Peter moved from a school for severely subnormal children to a local primary school. He copied the other children in everything and if he did not really do the reading and writing and arithmetic, he looked at the books and behaved as they did. When he had become used to the routine, the teacher gave him exercises he could do and he learned what he could learn. Peter's schoolfellows learned not only compassion for his disabilities, but also an appreciation of his gentleness and good humour. They laughed because he put his hand up every time the teacher asked a question but they were excited and pleased every time he mastered a new skill. Peter will have to transfer to a local special school when he is eleven; but it will be a school of his mother's choice to suit his need.

The right or the wrong school can become a central issue in adoption when children have special needs and require special provision. But even when adopted children go to ordinary schools and are bright like Hannah, they are very likely to require special consideration.

Hannah's parents tried to make sure that the headmistress and class teacher in the village primary school understood what adoption meant for Hannah. They explained that her life had been very fragmented and drew attention to the discrepancies between her age and her general knowledge. They were pleased that Hannah was treated with patience when she got into a muddle and was given the encouragement she needed – eventually Hannah began to want to learn.

Hannah, who could not show her feelings, wanted to show her schoolwork to her parents, but this was a school which did not allow children to take work home during term. Her parents told her that they were looking forward to the end of the school year when she could bring it all home. They promised to put the pictures up in the kitchen and to make a book of her stories.

On the last day of term Hannah came home late and upset and apparently making up excuses for not bringing her year's work with her. It was not good enough, the teacher had said 'no', there had been a fire, she had put it in a black bag, she did not know, understand, want to know or care. Her father rang the school. Yes, it was all in order, said the headmistress, they had given each child a black bag for all their writing and drawing and sums and they had had a bonfire in the garden which the children had enjoyed. No of course, they had not burnt the children's work, the black bags had gone with the rubbish. She did not like the children to bring their work home, she explained, because parents so often misunderstood what the teachers were trying to do. So without a thought and not unkindly, another part of Hannah's life, a whole year of school work, was cut off from her for ever as she saw it go off with the rubbish or go up in flames. Further proof of impermanence and worthlessness, just as her parents were trying to prove to her that she was valued and secure.

As children spend nearly half their waking hours in school, teachers, and what is taught and how, must be a telling factor in adoption. James' teacher became so interested in building families that she got the whole class working on a project about their own family patterns. James did not feel singled out because there was hardly a child in the group with a straight-forward family history. There were single parents, divorced parents, re-married parents, step-sisters, half brothers, other foster children and adopted children, children living with aunts or grandparents, children with cousins in every street in town and only children without any cousins at all. The way teachers tackle race, family life, language, people and places will influence all children, but it will matter more to adopted children who cannot measure up against a whole or solid framework of standards absorbed since birth. Their framework wobbles with uncertainty and struts are missing at essential points. Parents alone cannot rebuild this basic structure, if their child spends half of life at school, so it is vital that teachers help to make it a cohesive and comprehensible whole. But the framework cannot be treated as delicate forever and children have to learn to hold on tight.

It is self evident, but cannot be stressed often enough, that adopted children are not adopted first and children by the way, but that they are children who happen to be adopted. It is hardly helpful if teachers, or for that matter anyone at all including parents, are so aware of the child's status that they treat her as adopted rather than as a child. This happened to Dawn. At first the school protected her from anything that might be painful or embarrassing and later every inexcusable piece of behaviour was excused because she was adopted. Until it got too much to bear and then they had to start all over again with the real child before them and the real child was in trouble.

Services for families who have an emotionally handicapped child differ widely from one area to another but will, like schools, help to make or ruin a placement. Nick who came from a therapeutic boarding school was offered preventive therapy together with his new family so that he could attend an ordinary school and feel safe. Other families have had to wait until crisis followed crisis before help was made available and then there were further delays because there was a waiting list, forms had to be completed and the case allocated. Some parents have found family therapy most supportive because it confirmed them as a working unit and others have appreciated that child guidance offers a private place and a confidential ear to their child who may sometimes need to get away from the new family.

Many adopters wish that more psychologists and psychiatrists and therapists concerned themselves specifically with the issues raised by adoption. There are some, and families travel long distances to consult with them, but it is not possible to have regular treatment a hundred miles from home. Conventional therapy has sometimes made adopters angry because they feel they are made responsible for their child's behaviour when they are seeking advice about behaviour that came ready made with their child. The educational psychologist who saw Nick and his family told his parents that they were the only therapy Nick needed now. It would be comforting to believe that the same could be true for all children who are adopted when they are older and emotionally disturbed, but it would also be foolish.

Physically and mentally disabled children and their families need a range of support services whether they are adopted or not. Biological parents are worn out by their handicapped children, if the services do not provide relief. There is no reason to suppose that because parents choose to have a handicapped child they can or want to go it alone.

Handicapped children need everything more, not less, than ordinary children. Good medical care, playgroups, nursery schools, toys, space, education, training in due course, work and appropriate housing. The parents of handicapped children need the very best the health services and social services and voluntary agencies can offer and we really must ask the parents what that should be. Standard services are only for standard children and there are not many of those.

Relief can come in many guises. Bridgid would like to have a helper who would meet Margery from the school bus, give her tea and put her to bed once a week, while Robin's single mother would like an experienced responsible person to sleep in one day a fortnight so that she need not get up in the night when Robin wakes, shouts and does not go back to sleep. Jenny's family would like to have a local working and living scheme for multiply handicapped adults and Ben's family would like to have financial safeguards for his future. Diane and Louise's parents would like a washing machine and every gadget available to ease the daily chores, but they do not want any help with their children. Peter's mother wants nothing at all, at least for the time being.

Families may not use respite care facilities for years but they should know that relief is available for a few hours, a day, or a week when they want it. Leah is a bright little girl with spina bifida. Both her parents have to work until seven some evenings and Leah is getting too big to take around with them. The only place they can leave her where she will be safe is in a centre for severely subnormal adults. Leah does not like it there and her parents hate having to leave her. The staff in charge have made a complaint about the parents. They say that it is cruel and neglectful to leave Leah in the Centre even for a few hours and that the parents should not have adopted her if they cannot now look after her. They seem to be saying that if children need more than parents, and if whatever they need is not available, then they should not have parents either.

This kind of attitude can push biological parents to despair. They may already have been made to feel ashamed of producing an abnormal child and now they are accused of not caring and not providing. They may have to give up the struggle in anger and separate from their child. It is one of the strengths of adoptive parents of disabled children that they cannot be defeated by guilt. Leah's parents purposefully chose to have a spina bifida daughter and they will not easily give up the fight for suitable help which should be theirs by right.

Do we ever have to say that we cannot place with parents because 'parents are not enough'? We do sometimes have to say that we cannot place a child with a specific condition in an area where there are no facilities to treat that condition. We have to say that we cannot place a child in a district where there is no school for such a child because we believe that boarding school is hardly ever a desirable solution; parents who adopt do not usually want a part-time child and children who need adoption usually need more than a part-time family. We have to say that we cannot place a severely disabled child with parents who live an isolated life and who do not have friends and relations or a compassionate community to support them. We have to say that we cannot place a child with a family which is at loggerheads with every service their child will need to use. We do want parents to be ready to fight for their child but we do not want parents who make everything into a fight because then no one will be willing to work for them or with them. This is what we feel we must say and we say it, but families have persuaded us that they can overcome and we have watched them do it.

Josephine was placed in a rural area in East Anglia, with not one of the special facilities she needs. Her parents regularly and cheerfully take her to three different teaching hospitals in London, each dealing with particular aspects of her very complex medical condition. Schooling for a delicate, blind, non-speaking four-year-old was created for her in the local special school by an enlightened staff working closely with the determined but co-operative parents. The Health and Social Services, who were at first appalled by the very idea of our placing such a handicapped child in their midst and with such an unusual family, responded magnificently and Josephine has what her parents ask for: the very best. Now they are preparing to see if they can get the same for Sheeraz.

But adopters are not wizards and one placement, very early on, ended tragically mainly because a fourteen-year-old, educationally subnormal girl was out of school with no prospects of ever getting into a school again. It was not a question of not working hard enough to find a school that would take her – not even a boarding school could be found – and home tuition, a statutory requirement if a child is out of school, only provided for four hours teaching a week. Her distraught parents, worn out by the unending demands of the present and the dismal way ahead, could neither let go nor hold on hard enough – until they reached their breaking point. Even then they only intended to go away for a rest without their new daughter and they asked us to find a holiday home for her. It was a two week holiday but the girl, now a young woman, is still in that holiday home which finally became her own home with her own family.

On the other hand, Edward's mother knew that she would not find a suitable school for a fifteen-year-old with serious learning difficulties and did not try. She said she would teach him herself if we placed him with her and the education authority was only too relieved and so were we. Where could she have found a school for an apparently normal young adult who needs to go back to normal school work at an infant school level?

If parents on their own are not enough, they may become more effective in groups. In some places parents have got together in powerful unison to improve the services for their children and the groups have stayed together to offer mutual support and companionship. Most areas already have associations for adoptive families and for families with a handicapped child and pressure groups of many kinds. Parents have to use their energies according to their children's needs.

But we do not always know what a child needs. Nick had learning difficulties and was assessed as needing special education. Because he was only eleven when he was referred to us, we knew it was vital to find him a family in an area where there was the right kind of school for him. Nick wanted a large family, wanted to be fostered and needed a very special school. We could have taken for ever looking for the right family in the right place with the right school and we did look too long, for Nick was twelve by the time he was placed. He is being adopted now and will be an only child and in spite of other possibilities he goes happily to the local comprehensive school. Parents may not be enough, but they stretch a very long way. They may not make magic, but they do make families. We must make sure that we know what they need to keep going. And if they believe in the impossible, we have evidence that the impossible happens. Bridgid has a poster up in her hall to remind her of the tasks ahead. It is a photograph of a woman alone in an overcast and hilly countryside. 'Today I'm just blowing away the clouds,' she is saying, 'tomorrow I'll start moving the mountains.'

16   What's the Problem?

At the end of our first year an American colleague joined us
for six months as part of her Master's Degree in Social Work.
She was an experienced adoption worker herself, used to
different ways, but eager to understand ours. She made us
look, through her eyes, at what we did and why and how we
did it. We learned to value her questioning style, but one day
we were working out how we could possibly manage to fit one
more thing into an already overloaded day and, because her
own energy was boundless she asked, 'What's the problem?'
She was not being funny and we did not feel like laughing at
the time, but 'what's the problem?' has become a traditional
phrase to defuse the build-up of tension caused by overwork,
critical situations, high risks or needless delays. It also reminds
us that one person's problem is another's way of life and that
what we think is going to be a problem a family may take in its
stride, while we can be amazed by the problems that do arise.

   When is a problem not a problem? When the family does
not know it is there. Lily and Bob Dale have absorbed Fay
into their family as though she were a new born healthy baby
and not a thirteen-year-old Down's syndrome child who has
to learn everything about families as a baby would. It is not a
problem for them that they have broken nights because Fay
gets up and comes to their bedroom to make sure they are
there and has to be taken back to her own room and tucked up
before she will go to sleep again. It is not a problem for them
that she has to go to a special school, that she cannot go out of
the house on her own or be left in it without constant supervision. No more is it a problem that she cannot speak well, that
she will never be independent or ever do her share of family
chores. When the family went shopping, Fay wanted some of

everything and would not stop moaning until she had her own plastic carrier full of things. So now Lily and Bob give Fay a bag full of her own things to carry before they start out and it works. Another family could be driven crazy with irritation by such things, but Lily and Bob Dale are not.

On the other hand the Dales could have had problems with Nick, a more typical teenager who needed firm handling because he is afraid of his own violent feelings. He would not get up in the mornings and became aggressive when his new parents insisted. After due warnings they picked him up bodily from his bed one day and dumped him in the bath with his pyjamas on and doused him with cold water. He retaliated and turned the shower on his Mum and Dad. They were soaked, the bathroom was flooded, they all began to laugh and as they and the bathroom became wetter, they laughed more and more. Violence was safely contained and parents and child shared the making of a piece of family history which has been hilariously told and retold; no problem.

Even when parents agree there is a problem it does not necessarily take on the outlandish proportion we envisage when the child is placed. Blind, three-year-old Josephine picked. She picked at her clothes until they unravelled or became a series of holes. She picked at her bedding until it was in shreds and she picked at the sofa and armchairs like a destructive kitten. Her soft toys were a sad naked heap because the fur on them was especially tempting. When Josephine went home with her new parents she was still picking and they tackled the picking first because they knew they could not live with it. They simply did not let her pick. They stayed with her every waking moment and stopped her picking by giving her something to do. They did not feel that a blind child should behave any less well than a sighted one and they were very strict. If she did escape their vigilance and picked they were cross with her and if she started to pick and stopped when they told her, they rewarded her. It took a month and then it was over. It became a problem of the past, where it belonged.

We speak of problem children, of institutionalised children, of children who are maladjusted and emotionally handicapped.

We do not mean that these children are not normal children, what we do mean is that children who have been badly hurt may think that they have been hurt because they are bad, and so they feel bad and may need to show us just how bad they can be. They are not problem children, but they are children with problems.

These children come into new families with a backlog of failed relationships or unsatisfying relationships and they have no reason to suppose that really and truly it will be different this time round. In fact their expectations of being loved were higher when they were infants and they have become cynical with age. However well adjusted they may seem to be when they join a family, we can be sure that there will be some unfinished business lurking around, relating to their life in care. There will, very likely, be a honeymoon period while they manage to be, for a little while, the children they would like to be and feel they ought to be. But sooner or later they will act out their anxieties, test out where the limits are and find out whether they are really wanted, if they have the courage, or withdraw further into themselves if they have not.

Barbara was described as a thief and certainly when I met her, aged eleven, she was not too sure about what was hers and what was not. We had to warn adopters that Barbara would steal to test out their reaction. And we could share with them our understanding of how stealing had become a habit for her. When Barbara was five years old she longed for approval. She had no experience of family life and she wanted to impress her new foster parents, so when she saw a juggler on television and realised that they thought he was clever, she said, 'I can do that'. But the foster parents said she was lying. So Barbara became more desperate to impress them and was soon saying that she could do just anything at all. She could not understand that the foster parents were disapproving not of her, but of lying. After a time it did not seem to matter what she said because she felt disapproval anyway and often it was easier to lie than to tell the truth. As Barbara could not get close to her foster parents, she comforted herself by having some of their personal belongings close to her. She took things: a ring, a scarf, and a lipstick from her mother and money from her father and so she became known as a thief.

Trevor, who 'acted out', did everything a child can do to vex his adoptive parents. Other children vex their parents too, but not many nine-year-olds have such a repertoire of parent traps. Trevor wet the bed and when the mattress was covered with a rubber sheet, he wet the walls and the floor. He played truant from school. He took food from the fridge which he knew his mother wanted for tea and he took sweets and toys from shops. He provoked and bullied younger children and he tried to relate sexually to older ones. He dug up the flowers and the lawn and he told the sort of lies that got other people into trouble. He swore at his mother and father in public. If the family ever managed to enjoy a day together, Trevor had to spoil it all at the end because he felt bad and could not allow himself to be rewarded for being good. Just as one awful phase seemed to be over another would start. His mother was an agent for a mail order business. One day Trevor got the scissors and opened up one of her parcels and went on cutting until all the clothes were in shreds. He had to find out which was more precious: the mail order business or himself.

Children who have been damaged do not feel very precious. They cannot believe that they really matter and they may physically damage themselves to prove it. Excessive nail biting until the blood flows, deliberate bruising and self inflicted wounds are not uncommon, but it is dreadful to watch a child who has been hurt make it hurt more.

Children who love animals excessively because they do not easily relate to people, can also be cruel to pets when they feel angry with the parents they dare not love and fear to harm. One sweet looking little girl was placed with parents who bred rabbits and rabbits were found squeezed to death. Beloved dogs have been tormented until they howled and one cat ended up in the washing machine. Or children may withdraw with only an animal for company. It sounds quite charming for a boy to be his dog's best friend. But it is hard to live with a child who will only talk to and be spoken to through his dog, however therapeutic that may be. A tired parent at the end of the day does not want to tell the dog to tell the boy to clean his teeth. Especially if the boy is cut off in every other way too and will only speak if he has a blanket over his head.

Ted spoke a lot and he was very much present in his large and adolescent body in his new home, but his feelings and his thoughts were not with him, let alone with his family. He was emptied out as it were and somehow he had put a lid on tight so that nothing could get in. Emotions and thoughts did not penetrate and he had none to show. But he was very prone to breaking bones, was quite engrossed with himself and showed disproportionate concern for every scratch and pimple on his body. Even a flea bite was a matter of importance. 'What will happen now?' he asked as he watched the tiny swelling and it itched.

When children cannot negotiate relationships directly they may become preoccupied with alternative ways of getting care. If they are healthy they will demand it and clamour for it and be labelled as attention seeking. If they are less robust they will find other and more devious means.

All these problems we can anticipate because they have happened before and they crop up again and again. If a family is prepared for bedwetting, even three bedwetters at once have been managed with a new automatic washing machine and country space to hang out six sheets every morning. If parents understand that their child steals and that taking things is a substitute for taking love, they are not likely to be morally outraged the first time he is caught. But however well prepared and understanding families may be, they are not going to know how it feels to have three wet beds to change before breakfast until they are living with it or how unnerving it can be not to be able to trust your child with your belongings. And then problems could be problems yet. However, at worst, there is hope, even if it is the merest glimmer at the end of a very long tunnel, that lying, stealing, wetting, soiling and the whole range of disturbing behaviour will improve; for as it can be seen to be happening it is imaginable that it will stop. What perplexes many parents more are the intangible difficulties which do not have a name, which are less dramatic and which children do not know they make.

It does not seem to matter what other problems very young children bring with them or how handicapped they are as long as the parents can get enough sleep. A discontented, sleepless infant causes more stress to adopters than the most alarming medical condition. There is indeed something relentlessly rejecting about a baby which cries constantly in its new cot, in its lovingly prepared new room; or about the toddler who will not be comforted by her new parents. Who would not feel desperate to escape into sleep faced by an unhappy and un-satisfied small child with the power to make parents feel useless?

Children over school age bring other hard to define troubles. Adopters say that they are unpredictable, that they lack con-centration and spontaneity and that they take everything literally. Parents feel uneasy because they do not know what their child is thinking and there is unexplained tension over sexual development and greed.

It is most irritating to have a child around who cannot occupy himself and who, like Selwyn, complains if he is left unattended. If a toddler follows Mum everywhere including the bathroom, she can ignore him and guess that he will grow out of it, but Selwyn at ten could make life perpetually uncomfortable for the adults around him. Not because he had behaviour problems, but because he could not stay in one place or concentrate on what he was supposed to be doing. Or at least he could concentrate fairly well on Monday but not at all on Tuesday.

Selwyn was a bright boy who could still get by on his bad days, but Marion could not even open a cereal packet if she was not concentrating. And her unpredictable ability to con-centrate made her quite unreliable so that she could not be left unsupervised at any time.

We all know children who, we say, have grasshopper minds, but they are not all like Selwyn, who would say, 'What shall I do now?' every five minutes, or like Marion who would per-suade her mother that she could not do today what she could manage perfectly well yesterday, or like Hannah, who could not always remember what she was told because she could not always concentrate long enough to listen and her parents never knew if she had heard them. It is hard to be a child who has not had the opportunity to build up the confidence needed for concentration but it is also hard to be that child's family and not know where the child's thoughts have flown.

Parents do not and certainly should not mastermind their children. Our thoughts are our own unless we choose to share them and children also have this right to internal privacy. But parents generally know the range of their children's thoughts. Thoughts which must be based on experience which has, to some extent at least, been monitored by the parents.

If parents allow a small child to watch violence on television they are not surprised if that child is afraid to go to bed after the programme is over, has nightmares next week and writes about killing at school. They may consequently avoid violence on television when the child is up, or they may decide that the child needs to know the world. Either way they would be prepared for a certain set of responses. They may be angry if friends allow their child to see a forbidden programme, but the chances are they would know if it had been watched; they may not approve of what grandma said to the child, of the school's attitude to sport, of the best friend or of sweets, but they would have some idea of what their child was doing, feeling and seeing so that his thought processes would not be completely strange to them. Even when children go away to relatives, to boarding schools or on holiday with their own friends, parents at least think they know what is involved. When children past infancy are adopted, parents cannot begin to know what is in their minds.

Families have told us that it is uncanny to have a child who has had experiences they have not shared, especially if those experiences are known to have been unpleasant or tragic. No official record, however well it conveys the facts, can convey the quality of Nick's experiences and reactions. His adoptive parents have no way of knowing for certain whether going to the zoo will awaken memories of aggression or of feeding the lions. Whether a bad dream refers back to fears of long ago or to a fear of school tomorrow. Whether a blank stare hides a reluctance to voice an opinion about a current situation or a preoccupation with a situation in the past.

What does 'illness' in the family mean to Margery in the wheelchair who has already experienced the death of a mother? What does 'hospital' mean to James who had six major operations before he met his 'forever' family? What does 'Surbiton' mean to Sandra who lived there for six years as though she were someone else? Adoptive parents do not know whether and when their new child is thinking of a lost sister, a lost toy or a lost baby blanket and anyway they would not know what the blanket, the toy and the sister were like. So even if children do speak their thoughts, parents may be able to do no more than to nod and accept. It is a foreign inner world the adopted child brings into a family, and it cannot but remain a lonely world for the child and a mysterious one for the parents.

One of the most dispiriting characteristics of children who have been in care is their lack of spontaneity. The family outing especially arranged to please the new child may draw scarcely a comment or what could seem like very formal praise from a ten-year-old. Hannah always made a pretty speech which left her parents wondering if she had enjoyed herself. A telling off may produce no response at all, an accident to another member of the family a callous silence and a visitor from the past can come and go without any apparent effect on the child.

Margery in the wheelchair seemed to miss her ex-house-parents. Her new mother, wanting to get everything right, invited them with some trepidation in case the visit upset Margery more than it pleased her. As far as one could tell it did not do either.

Nick's pride was apparently his adopted swan in a wildlife park near to his previous boarding school, but a very long way from where he is living now with his parents. Nevertheless his mother made the necessary effort to take him there one fine Sunday. She loved the place and was fascinated by the birds, but Nick was bored almost as soon as they got there and wanted to turn back and come home.

Even more discouraging is the child who cannot spontaneously say she is sorry, or if she says it, does not know how to mean it. The child who cannot show remorse is not easy to embrace. Wanting to repair the damage we have done is one of our human triumphs, and a basic requisite for making relationships. As infants we learn that our fury can be safely held by loving parents and that however much we transgress we can be pardoned. The child who cannot make reparation has not learnt that anger need not destroy, that she can be forgiven. It is the saddest, as well as the most maddening flaw for parents to endure.

All parents have to endure their children's adolescence. There is usually anxiety during adolescence about the sexual development of disabled children and there is a fair amount of anxiety around the sexual development of older adopted children, handicapped or not.

Will disabled children develop normally and be able to have children of their own or would it be better if they could not? Should mentally retarded girls be put on the pill? Will mentally retarded boys be sterile or impotent or both or neither? Should handicapped adult women and men be encouraged and indeed helped to have sexual relations? Looking at Jill and Ben and at Robin and Josephine these questions seem premature but for Margery and Marion, both soon leaving school, the issues are pressing.

Will children adopted when already adolescent or nearing puberty relate appropriately to their new sisters and brothers and mother and father? Will they be sexually provocative within the family or be at risk from strangers outside it? Children who have not had enough love may seek it and accept it sexually in an unsuitable way they themselves do not comprehend. Children who have been sexually assaulted may provoke further abuse.

Even if a family talks easily about sex and the feelings that go with it, most mothers find it hard to acknowledge that they are jealous of their adopted daughter's sexuality and fathers may get into confrontations with their adopted sons if they seem to be rivals for the affections of the mother. In home grown families these conflicts have a chance of being resolved in early childhood, but if children are adopted later and especially if one or both of the adoptive parents are infertile then the situation can become explosive.

One mother got to the point when she could not allow her adopted daughter to come into the kitchen because, she said, she flaunted herself as a better woman than her parent. She was a better cook, a better housekeeper and, the implication seemed to be, would be a better wife given the opportunity. Ernie's first introductions partly failed because he was daily growing taller and stronger and more blatantly masculine than his sensitive, quiet father-to-be. It takes a tough, deep and giving marital relationship to counter these kinds of threats.

All children exploit the chinks in their parents' armour but usually they have a vested interest in keeping their parents together. Older children without family experience do not necessarily have that same interest. Doris liked the first couple we introduced her to but she wished they would separate because she only wanted to live with the mother and the baby. Doris, like many children in care, instinctively feared that she would not be able to relate to more than one adult at a time. Trying to split parents up, getting it where it hurts with an unfailing nose for the weakest spot, these are not endearing qualities, but neither are they deliberately intended to demolish the family the child wants to have. They are the clumsy and misguided overtures of children who do not understand relationships and lack the skill to make them.

Such children take things literally. Their imagination is no poorer than other children's, indeed they are likely to have a rich fantasy life, but they take what is said to them quite literally because their language is impoverished. A profusion of misunderstandings follow. So, 'You'd better choose the blue one to show you're a boy', said five years ago about a sweater means that the burly teenager will only wear blue in case he is mistaken for a girl. 'Mum doesn't like bread' means Mum must not eat bread in any circumstances, 'Dad is always late' means he has to give an account of himself if he comes home on time, 'you'll never get a job' seals a fate of lifelong unemployment and 'I'm saving it for a rainy day' means watch out, for whatever it is will be found and solemnly produced when the rains come. Every family has a tale to tell about the misunderstandings that have followed their child's literal understanding. Most of the anecdotes are amusing and fondly remembered, but in the long run it is irritating either to explain the meaning behind the meaning, or to avoid anything but basic language; it makes it harder to treat life with humour and without humour it can become grim.

Food also has its grim aspect for families. The children they adopt are often greedy and eating becomes a battle. A silent battle with Keith who will not ask for more and is given all that he needs, but less than he wants. A noisy battle with Emily who just goes on and on stuffing herself until she should get fat or sick but somehow does not. Greed can be nauseating to watch and to live with and hurtful when children substitute food for love.

We are no longer surprised when families find it hard to be relaxed about food. Even families who have handled their children wonderfully well in all other respects have made an issue about having more than one biscuit after school or having to choose between an apple or a bun at tea-time. Naturally some families are large and there may not be enough to go round and other families cannot afford more than the essentials, but these are not the families, in our experience, who mind if their new children overeat. It has more to do with a puritanical, self punitive streak in some families who perhaps feel that they have too much of everything good. Or it may be that children act out the greed adults control, and parents do not want to see something in their children that they have conquered in themselves.

When parents have been easy going about food, children's appetites have found their normal level more quickly. James was described as very greedy by the family who could not keep him and it bothered them that he would eat anything and everything, indiscriminately. We warned his new parents not to leave food about because James would gobble it up. But they were not going to treat James any differently from their five other children who all helped themselves to fruit, biscuits, crisps and drinks whenever they felt like it. As the mother is a good cook and the children liked their meals they did not eat much in between. At first James could not believe his luck and the thin little boy who had arrived began to burst out of his clothes. All the time he was at home he was chewing and, if the rest of the family thought it was odd, they did not think it was bad. A year later James was back to his wiry self and now he is so busy with his younger brother and baby sister and school friends and cubs and just being a member of that bustling family that he hardly has time to stop for a drink when he comes home from school.

Nick's parents handled greed as they handle everything else, with the most amiable humour. Nick took to drinking up all the milk in the house and boasted that he would drink a pint down without stopping for breath, and he showed that he could. So they congratulated him and bought him his very own pints and made sure there were always some waiting for him to drink down in one go. Nick drank a lot of milk during his first few months with them and occasionally he still likes to make sure there is enough for him, but now he will always ask his mother whether she can spare it.

Good humour is the very best antidote to problems and parents have an easier time with their adopted, hard to place children, if they can find a funny side as Nick's parents could. They followed the cold bath and the pints of milk with 'The Heavy Hand'. They want to have a son who is sociable and well behaved, but it is not in their nature to nag or to be heavy-handed. Instead they have developed the idea of 'The Heavy Hand' which knows all and follows Nick around and leaves him notes pinned up in surprising places to remind him to clean the basin, to make his bed, to feed the fish, to do the washing up. Every note has an outline of 'The Heavy Hand' with approximate weight. And the Hand grows heavier if Nick grows more careless. Another family joke, a private ritual which draws parents and child closer together and gets results.

But when Nick helped himself to his mother's money no one laughed. His parents were not taken aback, but they communicated their serious disapproval and thought out the best way for Nick to make amends. They stopped his pocket money knowing full well that Mother's Day was coming up and that Nick had planned to go shopping with his father. Now, instead, his father encouraged him to make a card and to give his mother a special day without a present. Nick gladly accepted his mother's unconditional pleasure with his unmaterial offerings and he was left in no doubt that he and his offerings were valued, but he was also left in no doubt about his parents' attitude towards stealing.

What we see as a problem or foresee, what families know to be problems and what children experience as problems is not what adoption is about, as the people who are adopting constantly remind us. Selwyn's mother who is also Sandra's mother and the mother of twelve others, who has coped with every problem we have ever imagined, gets quite cross and cool with us if we dwell on them instead of acknowledging the gifts these problematic children bring. Even while Selwyn would only refer to her as 'it' and refused to touch any food she prepared and lost every piece of clothing she bought for him, his mother was more aware of his hurt, of his tentative trust, of his uncertain loving and of his courageous battle for his place in her heart, and in the world. In his family it is a case of count your blessings and the problems will look after themselves, with a lot of very skilled help from the mother and many well disposed friends and relations.

We hope that we can also help. We can and do help to explain the child's present behaviour in terms of his life in care. We can and do share again the child's file because it will mean more two years later than it did during the tense period of preparation. When progress stops, we can and do remind families of the progress that has already been made because sometimes we are the only people who can remember what the problems were at the beginning. We can, and hope that we do, give parents the confidence they need to believe and to go on believing that their child is better off with them than in the Children's Home, the foster home, the nursery or even with the natural family as things turned out. It can be devastating for parents who are giving their all to be made to feel that all is not good enough, and children are experts at doing this.

Families talk with us about the problems and work with the tools we offer. After Marion recovered from her mysterious illness she could not orientate herself. She could not remember the sequence of her life leading up to her illness, nor could she grasp where she was now in relation to where she had been. This is always a problem for children whose lives are without apparent consequence; Keith at eleven could not tell the time, Hannah had no concept of the day after tomorrow, Sandra thought South East London was unconnected to the North West which she knew, and Marion, even before her illness, had not been able to comprehend how people came in and out of her life and went on existing elsewhere. We made a story book for Marion with clear bright pictures and short warm words. It was her own story and she made it hers because she learned it by heart, every word and every detail of every illustration. If her mother teased her and read it wrong,

Marion would laugh and say, 'No, it wasn't like that, it wasn't there, it was like this and it was here.' This was a good tool and we have made others to help parents to help their children, but afterwards we have gone to our own homes and left the parents in theirs with the children we have placed with them.

We understand that it matters more that the children are wanted than that they were placed. We know that the families who adopt them are problem solvers and will draw on their own life experiences to solve many more. Bridgid said that she felt like a wounded healer with her children and that having lived through her own darkness she could live with theirs. We can only give her our confidence and wonder what we would answer if our American friend should come back and ask again: 'What's the problem?'

17 Money

Adopters do not need favours, but they have the same financial needs as other families and should enjoy at least the same benefits. Geoffrey's mother, who had worked for ten years in a day nursery and was a matron by the time she and her husband adopted Geoffrey, calculated that she lost £300 in maternity benefits because she adopted a handicapped child instead of giving birth to a normal baby. That was in 1978 and the loss increases with inflation. According to the 1958 Adoption Act: 'it shall not be lawful to make or give to any person payment or reward for or in consideration of (a) the adoption by that person of an infant.' This made sense when adoption was primarily a service for childless couples and it was considered that a white healthy baby brought its own rewards to parents with an adequate income. The people who come forward to adopt older and handicapped children are more likely to be parents already; they may be adding to one child, to many children or they may be starting a second family when their own has grown up. They may be single parents or handicapped themselves. What these potential adopters have in common is not a high standard of living which will stretch, but room for one more.

It is traditional for foster parents to have a regular boarding out allowance and to claim for extras such as clothes, holidays, and piano lessons. It is often suggested when we ask for grants for our adoptive parents that if they cannot afford to adopt, they should become foster parents instead. This view completely disregards the difference between adoption and fostering and does a disservice to both. Foster care is not adoption second class and if foster care is proposed it should be because foster care is what the child needs and what the parents offer. Foster care includes a whole range of services for children: emergency care during a time of family crisis, supplementary care which involves the child's own family, shared long term care with the local authority for children who are not expected to return to their own family but who cannot and should not be adopted, and professional foster care for children who need to experience family life as part of a treatment plan. None of these options include taking total responsibility for a child, or having the rights and the legal obligation of natural parents. Foster parents perform the task of looking after other people's children as though they were their own, adoption provides children with families which become their own and families are for life. The child in a foster home remains in care, the adopted child does not. It is no good placing a child to be fostered with a family which only wants to adopt or placing a child with a foster family in the hope that they will adopt in time. They may, but it is not what they asked for in the first place.

Lily and Bob Dale do not have enough money to bring up another disabled child, but they are still the best family we could have found for Fay. They do not want to stand in for Fay's parents nor do they want to be paid for a service. They want to build their family, and they want to have an allowance that will enable them to become Fay's parents by adoption.

The 1975 Children Act brought in legislation which came into effect for an experimental seven year period in February 1982 and which will give the Dales what they want. The Approved Adoption Allowance is something akin to an enhanced Child Benefit, but is administered and paid by the Social Services. Under the act local authorities have wide powers to tailor each scheme to the needs of each family. It is meant to ensure that hard to place children like Fay, Sandra, Sheeraz or Edward, will not miss out on adoption because of financial reasons. Critics of the scheme rightly point out that it would have been wise to spend as much money and more on keeping the family together in the first place. However, keeping a child in care is even more costly and if families have irreversibly broken down, it is surely wise to spend money on replacing the parents the child has lost.

The Approved Adoption Allowance can be paid when the child is placed and be continued after legal adoption until the child is eighteen. But even this can be varied and one London borough is making an open ended commitment to Sheeraz whose adoptive family may need financial support for longer if she does not become an even partially independent adult. School fees will be included for Sandra who is doing well at her private school and Edward's mother could not have afforded the time and the materials to teach him at home without a special allowance.

How much a family needs is a question of how they perceive need. The Approved Adoption Allowance could be awarded to a family which asks for it and needs it, but may have a bigger income than the next family which does not want to have it. Attitudes towards money and need are intensely personal and there is no way of measuring what is fair. It seems fair that Sandra's mother will have enough for what her family regard as comfortable living, whereas the Dales will have less because they pride themselves on getting by with very little. Sheeraz' family will be covered for expenses caused by her medical condition, but parents who adopt a Down's syndrome baby would most probably not qualify for an allowance at all because we would not be able to claim that a Down's syndrome baby could not be adopted without financial aid.

It is bad luck for parents who adopted when they could not easily afford to adopt, because the approved allowance cannot be awarded in retrospect. If families fostered because they needed the money, they can adopt now and go on receiving the same amount but if they went ahead and legalised the adoption it is considered that they could afford to do so, whether they could or not.

We managed to create an income for one child so that he could be adopted before the allowance became law. We knew that Selwyn was ready to be adopted by his single mother after three years of troubled conduct and that he would not be able to stay calm if there was going to be an indefinite delay. Encouraged by another social worker who knew Selwyn and shared our opinion, we formed a Parents for Children Trust Fund. Through the efforts of one determined business man on our behalf we raised enough money by covenant and private subscription for Selwyn to be maintained until he is eighteen. With the help of our legal adviser we made sure that the way it was paid would not contravene any part of the 1958 Adoption Act. And then Selwyn was adopted.

We have used the same Trust Fund to help Jenny and James' parents to adopt the latest addition to their family, Nina, the Down's syndrome baby. When Nina is two, like most disabled children, she will qualify for the Attendance Allowance, but her family could not have managed until then without some regular extra money. They did not want to postpone the adoption for two years, but they might have had to if the Trust Fund had not been able to provide the equivalent of the Attendance Allowance from the time Nina was placed with them. If Nina does not learn to walk or if she cannot later use public transport, she may also qualify for a Mobility Allowance when she is five. And then if her parents run a car they will be exempted from paying the vehicle excise duty or road tax.

There are grants apart from the Attendance and Mobility Allowances which are available to all parents of handcapped children. The local Social Services Department can be asked to pay the telephone rental, to pay for respite care and to pay for aids and adaptations in the home. The health service can be asked for a free pushchair, a wheelchair, a tricycle and a free nappy service. Families with a physically disabled child can apply for rate rebates and for special housing.

Other help is at hand. The government has set up 'The Family Fund' to help parents with extra expenses created by the needs of handicapped children and there are a variety of trusts and funds set up to help one parent families, adoptive families and ordinary families. Finally, for Parents for Children families, there is the Parents for Children Sponsors' Fund to help out with a holiday, a car repair, a telephone account or whatever it is that families need to have and cannot afford. Children are expensive, disabled children who need special care and older children who lose clothes and break things are even more expensive. Parents need money to bring up children and adoptive parents of hard to place children need more money. We encourage them to make the most of every available benefit.

If adopters can afford to accept full financial responsibility for their child we still negotiate a substantial grant when children are first placed. The amount varies with the age of child and the requirements of the family, but we keep in mind the maternity benefits available to biological parents and we expect the grant to cover at least the initial outlay for clothes and bedding and equipment. A car seat, a fire guard, a stair gate, a high chair and a cot are acquired gradually by natural parents but adopters will have to get them all at the same time if they are adopting a toddler. A new bicycle is probably waited and saved for by each of the children in turn in a large family, but it would be hard for an adopted child to start off without one when everyone else has one and cycling is the thing. Yet a bicycle as well as new clothes, a school uniform, bedding and football boots is more than most parents could bear unaided. And even if they could, we consider that the grant is a financial acknowledgement of their parenthood and they should be able to claim it just as they can claim the Child Benefit from the day the child joins the family.

If single men and women decide to become full time parents they can elect not to be wage earners while a dependent child is at school, but they will still qualify for full supplementary benefit rates from the time the child is placed for adoption. If the child is handicapped, Attendance and Mobility Allowances are not affected. Bridgid and her children have lived well on social security benefits and so have Robin and his mother, but it is not everyone's idea of the good life. One parent families do not have sufficient state support and adoptive one parent families do not fare any better, especially as it is hard to insist on all the extras that they are also entitled to: free school dinners and medicine, free travel to and from hospitals, heating and diet addition and special payments for special needs like moving house, buying more shoes than is normal when a child ruins a pair a month and more warm bedding because a disabled child feels the cold.

Personal money is not much talked about in Britain. It is all right to discuss the national income, the budget, the wage demands and income policies and price increases, but not how much a person has or earns. There is a certain feeling that it is not right to mix money and children, that the welfare of the child must obliterate all financial considerations, that there is something unclean about money and that both poverty and riches are better hidden out of sight.

In other European countries people are less reticent about what they do and how much they earn. Wage packets and salary slips are not highly confidential in the Middle East. In America money is of general interest and the few welfare benefits available are usually claimed, but here we become inhibited as soon as money is mentioned and we do not claim all the welfare benefits which are ours by right. Somehow it is generally thought that to ask for money is bad form even if that money is freely available.

We have worked with a father who would not claim Mobility Allowance for his immobile daughter because he felt it would be exploiting her handicap. We have worked with a mother who would not claim the child benefit due to her until weeks later because she felt it was mercenary to get all she could. We know that one non-earning single parent will not apply for the night Attendance Allowance because it would be making a fuss about having to get up to her disabled daughter in the early hours every morning. We try hard to convey that accepting grants, welfare benefits and allowances is not putting a material value on the child and that they are not charitable hand-outs. But because we are also inhibited about money, we probably do not emphasise this as well or as often as we should.

Some adopters will not need or want any financial support, some will need it and not want it and some will want it and not need it, but it all comes back to how they see themselves. We should not imply that material help is less important or less respectable than other kinds of help. Some people will always want more than others and it will not make them better or worse adopters; no one is likely to want to adopt for financial gain. Families need money, but money does not build families. Bridgid was fooling around with Margery when they came home after buying new clothes for spring. She took off all the price tags and stuck them on her forehead and said to Margery, 'How much am I worth?' Margery thought before she said, 'I don't know, I got you for nothing.'

18   Alternatives

We introduced Laura to two families before she moved in with a third. She stayed for six months. The family, her Children's Home staff and the Parents for Children workers were depressed, tired and pessimistic about the future, but Laura was fine.

Thelma met two families, she attacked the younger child of one and emptied the drawers of the other and neither could cope, but Thelma hardly seemed to notice and not to care at all. She came from the same Children's Home as Laura, she had been brought up with Laura and after each failed introduction or placement the two girls were only too pleased to go back to each other and Oscar in the only home the three of them had known. Oscar, like Laura and Thelma, was a multiply handicapped teenager waiting for a family. Oscar was referred to Parents for Children at a time when Laura and Thelma were with us again and we stopped trying to find families for any of them and looked at what had been happening and listened to what the people it happened to had to say.

Laura is the youngest of the three, partially sighted, epileptic and mentally retarded. Lack of oxygen during a difficult birth caused severe cerebral palsy. She has never known her father and her mother has never been able to look after her. At fourteen she was lively and friendly, had nice manners and spoke well, although her understanding and sense of humour were more like a five-year-old's. She could walk short distances with help, and loved pop music, simple jigsaws and lots of attention. She would present any family with a multiplicity of problems in day to day care.

The first family we found understood girls because they had several already and they knew about nursing care. They wanted Laura, could accept all her disabilities, could cope with her seizures, tablets, hospitals and dependency, but they could not tolerate her immodesty. Like any five-year-old Laura would unselfconsciously wear her pyjamas unbuttoned and leave the bathroom door open. It would have been wrong to make Laura feel worried about something she could not comprehend but it would also have been wrong to make the family accept behaviour that offended their sense of what was right and wrong.

We forewarned the second family about the emotional problems Laura seemed to have. Both parents worked with mentally handicapped adults and they were well prepared for a retarded child. But they were not prepared for the physical effort involved in meeting their own very young children from school with Laura in tow. They lived at the top of a steep hill without pavements and the daily walk endangered all three children. The mother could only hold on to two of them and she was exhausted every time Laura dragged on her for support up the hill or leant on her for safety coming down. The short distance between the village and their home, which they had always prized because it gave them privacy, now became an endurance test for the family and for Laura too. We tried to learn more from these parents about the needs of this multiply handicapped child so that we could get it right for Laura next time.

The next time it seemed to work. This third family could not be surprised by anything because they had brought up two handicapped boys of their own. Neither was as disabled as Laura, but the parents were confident that they could build on their experience and so were we. Laura seemed to be happy getting to know this family but she had been happy enough getting to know the others. She moved in without saying very much about it but everything went wrong from that moment.

Laura could not comprehend the meaning of permanence, adoption or family. She had always wanted a Mummy and Daddy like children want a baby doll or a train set because other children have them and talk about them. Laura could not settle in her new school and would not even try to master any new skills. She was constantly wanting to go back to the Children's Home to see Thelma and Oscar. She wanted to know what they had done at school and what they had eaten for tea and what they were watching on television. She could not tell the difference between coming to stay for a weekend treat and coming to stay for good except that this was going on a bit too long, as she kept telling us. The parents were hopeful that Laura would eventually get used to the change. They were certain that she could make the same kind of progress their sons had made in spite of the predictions of the experts. They persevered.

Laura did not get used to the change because she could not grasp the reason for it. Instead of making some progress to give her parents enough satisfaction to carry on, Laura came to a standstill and then regressed. After six months the family and Laura parted. The parents and their older children had made a huge emotional investment in taking Laura and they retreated wounded and guilty. Laura came back to the Children's Home as if after a long holiday. She went back to her old school and only wondered occasionally why her Mummy and Daddy did not come to see her. She could not appreciate that they found it too painful to keep up a casual relationship. If anyone asked Laura why she had not wanted to stay with her Mummy and Daddy she said she didn't like the way they washed her hair over the basin.

These parents came almost fourteen years too late for Laura. She could have been their daughter and they could have enjoyed her as much as they enjoyed their sons, but by the time they found her she could not understand what she had to gain while she knew what she had to lose! Thelma and Oscar, her family.

Thelma is the oldest of the trio and two years older than Laura. She is a big girl, not well co-ordinated and has a speech defect. Laura and Oscar can understand what she says and interpret for her but not everyone can. She was born with a chromosome abnormality which causes mental retardation, an unusual physical appearance and poor eyesight. She is a kind girl and the people who have taken care of her have always liked her. She shared Laura's wish for a Mum and Dad but had the same kind of trouble with comprehension. The two families who were introduced did not make much impression on her and mercifully they decided to withdraw before she was placed with them. For Thelma would also have moved in without a murmur and without being able to make the slightest commitment and she would also have been too old to take the change in her stride.

Oscar was the most difficult to handle of the three children. He is a good looking boy and physically well developed, but he was brain damaged at birth and his behaviour can be irrational and bizarre. He used to be obsessed by dogs, smoking and shaving. His fear of dogs made it unsafe for him to be out in the street for even if someone was holding on to him he would wrench himself away and run if he saw a dog. He refused to go anywhere new in case a dog lived there and if a dog did manage to come near him he went berserk.

Oscar's obsession with shaving was more endearing although he could make strangers nervous. Oscar had a goodly collection of discarded and obsolete razors and he knew a thing or two about them. He would go up to any man, and usually it was every man he met, and ask whether he had shaved that morning. If the unsuspecting man said yes, a knowledgeable barrage of questions would be fired at him about razors, hairs, soap and water. Some men were kindly whether they understood the situation or not, some men were offended and some had a sheepish embarrassed look because they probably thought they were being interviewed for television. Oscar provided the stuff that candid camera programmes are made of.

When he was not busy with shaving he was busy with cigarettes. He gave the most perfect imitation of smoking so that disapproving adults would start to tell him off before they saw that the rolled up paper dangling from his lips was empty or the butt being carefully put out in the ashtray was unlit. And he would ask quite seriously, 'Do you mind if I have a smoke?'

Oscar could be a delightful character but he could as easily be mean, rude and out of control. If Laura and Thelma had not been able to make the transition into a family how would Oscar? He was fifteen years old, disturbed and disturbing and he had no idea about relationships. Fathers, mothers, sons, daughters, sisters, brothers, and cousins were muddled up together and Oscar would say with equal conviction that the housemother was the cat's sister or that his teacher was either his wife or his mother.

So we took stock and we went back to the local authority in whose care these three children were. They told us that the children had to move because the Home, their Home, was closing down and we said that we could not place them with families, but we wondered whether a family could not be placed with them.

It made sense. Here were three adolescents who required some kind of family provision now and would need support as mentally handicapped adults always. And they were as much a family group as any family groups we had placed together. They related to each other in a way they related to no one else.

We had mistakenly regarded them as three disabled children living together by chance in the only Children's Home that would take handicapped babies more than a decade ago. We had known that the children were used to each other, but had not seen beyond to the signals of attachment. The way they stood up for one another, the way they turned to each other for approval, compensated for one another's handicaps and were aware of each other even when parted. If Laura went out to tea she would say which kind of biscuits Oscar liked best and ask for one for him and Thelma would make sure that everyone waited for Laura, and Oscar when he came back from an outing would ask first: 'Where's Laura? Where's Thelma?'

It would not have been within the bounds of sanity to try to recruit a family with the room, the stamina, the ability, the experience and the desire to take these three teenagers into their home and to adopt them. And, even if very specialised foster parents could have been found, that would not have been a permanent arrangement. So if the children could not join a family, a family would have to join them.

We therefore suggested that the local authority provide a suitable house and that it should be the children's house maintained from the generous allowances the authority was willing to make with security of tenure for each child for life. This simple project, in order to work, would need even more luck than good management. The good management was at hand in the Borough, but a family who would want to move in to take care of the children seemed a fantasy, even while we were affirming our faith in the belief that someone, some-where, was only waiting to be asked.

The housing department offered a five bedroomed unit on a new estate, (the Director of Social Services agreed to hold the tenancy until the children came of age) the children chose the furniture, the curtains and the carpets and everyone waited for the right family to turn up. A reliable, mature family, parents who were patient, confident and preferably with experience of a whole range of disabilities; a family ready and willing to uproot without any guarantee of permanence for it was always understood that the children would stay put and the family would move out if the arrangement did not work or if the parents did not want to continue it. It would be hard on the children if a family left and a new one came, but they would keep each other and their home.

The family came as soon as the house was ready. The parents already knew Thelma, Laura and Oscar because they had a mentally handicapped teenage son of their own at the same school. They wanted him to have more companionship and they wanted to be a large family and they could not see that living with four disabled teenagers was going to be all that odd or difficult. They had already brought up a normal family, but now they were interested in a handicapped one. They wanted to move anyway and the children's house was in the right place for them and they were unworried by the prospect that they might have to move again as the Borough undertook to rehouse them if the need arose.

Family and children moved in together and three years later it is hard to imagine that anyone will want to move out. The parents have become 'Mum and Dad' it seems for life, but the fairy story ending should not overshadow the aim of the project. Laura and Thelma and Oscar will always have security because a local authority acted with imagination and foresight and speed to place a family with children who could not, apparently, be placed with a family.

Adoption is not the only alternative for children unable to live with their biological families, but realistic and early planning is essential for each child.

As soon as children are referred to Parents for Children we

set up a discussion with all the people involved to consider each child's needs and what is available. Why adoption? What does the child know, think and feel about herself, her past and her future? How could the local authority find a family and what other provision does it offer? In this way we avoid a long waiting list of children who could not or should not be adopted: children who may not be free for adoption or who need a supplementary family rather than permanent substitute parents. Sometimes children are referred to us simply because their Children's Home is closing or a foster placement has broken down without any real consideration of the alternatives.

This first discussion, which we call a consultation day, usually takes a whole day and focuses on three children and their workers so that there is a general sharing of problems, ideas and practice. After each such day at least one of the group has said to us that they have never had an opportunity like this to explore the possibilities with their co-workers, seniors and adoption officers. The consultation day could even be the first time that field worker and residential worker or foster parent have had the chance to exchange views and grapple together with certain issues concerning their child. The one most often and most easily neglected is: who really works with the child, what for, how, when and where? Imaginative and creative plans have been made for children on these days and by no means every child initially referred to us has been placed for adoption.

A few children have gone or will go back to their own families – not necessarily to parents but to a grandmother or an uncle – after some new work to clear the way inspired by the joint discussion. For one child adoption would have been a disruption of a 'good enough' relationship with a retired housemother and it was decided to develop rather than terminate what the child already had. Some severely handicapped children were sadly assessed as too old to tolerate the change from institution to family. A more specialised and long term institution was the solution for one such teenager, while a promise to be able to stay in the Home where she was happy as a member of a stable group which would move on to a Home for adults together, was the plan for another. A multiply handicapped baby was getting the best care available in a small private unit in the country where he would be able to stay until he was eighteen except that he was unlikely to live that long. He would always need round the clock attention and the permanent nursing couple in charge wanted to keep him. We could only help them and the local authority to believe that they had done and were doing everything possible for this baby.

Amy was referred to Parents for Children as an act of desperation. She was fifteen and a half, totally blind and partially deaf. She was an orphan from the Far East, brought to England as a baby for adoption and rejected because she was handicapped. She rocked, bit and picked at herself until she bled. No one could measure her intelligence or understanding because no one could make any contact with her. Her ears were permanently festering so that she could not wear the hearing aids which were her only contact with the real world. Amy had lived for a long time in a mental subnormality hospital. A new social worker, a concerned psychiatrist and a nurse defeated by the system did not seriously consider that Amy could be adopted, but they just wanted to make something happen. All of us at that consultation day were horrified by her story.

Nothing will ever make up for Amy's deprivation but between us we came up with an idea that worked. Pressure was put on the local authority in whose care Amy was, to provide the funding for an experienced child care worker who would look after Amy in hospital on a one-to-one basis. Something was at last going to happen in Amy's life and as concern was focused on Amy's special needs more plans were made. She is now waiting to move into a small Home, purpose built to suit her and three other blind girls, where she will have very special care for the rest of her life.

Another child, a boy almost as handicapped as Amy and from a similar background, had other plans made for him. Hammett was left alone in this country when his young foreign mother died in hospital. She knew she was dying of cancer and asked a voluntary children's society to take care of her severely subnormal thirteen-year-old son. One particularly devoted worker became Hammett's substitute parent. Ursula struggled with Hammett to get him toilet trained, to teach him to feed and dress himself, to go to school and to learn sign language for he will never speak. Then Ursula came to Parents for Children to discuss Hammett's long term future because she wanted to adopt him to give him the security he needed and to give her the right to make decisions on his behalf, even if one day she has to decide to let him go into some kind of institutional care.

We agreed that Stella needed to be adopted. She really wanted parents and she knew what that meant, and she would have made an effort to be lovable and caring. It made it all the harder not to be able to provide them for we could not find a family for Stella. She was not an easy girl to place. She was fifteen years old and went to a special school for maladjusted girls. She ate refuse, soiled her pants and indulged in sexual fantasies about every man she met. She was also cheerful, chatty, brave and extremely kind, which was surprising considering her story.

Stella had been left in the reception area of a Social Services Department when she was ten because her foster parents were emigrating to Canada and said they could not take her. She had lived with them for as long as she could remember and thought they were her real parents. This total, abrupt abandonment affected her mind and the psychiatrist who advised our potential adopters could not give any reassurance about her future mental health even if her circumstances were changed. The risks were too great for the families who came forward. We failed Stella because we failed to find a family that would be prepared to take those risks and surely there is such a family. Just as there is Beatrice.

Beatrice is a single parent who already has a severely handicapped young son. He has to have nearly all his mother's attention and Beatrice would not have the time or the energy to look after another demanding child, but she had just enough to spare of both time and energy to become a part-time family for Stella. Stella can make her own way on public transport and she visits Beatrice and her son most weekends and sometimes she calls in during the week. She is grown up now and lives in a hostel with other teenagers who have been in care and need psychiatric treatment, but unlike most of them she has a family to turn to. It has not been enough for Stella's needs but it has given her a supplement, an alternative to family placement and an alternative to nothing.

Len also found an alternative solution through trial and error and luck. He is the Down's syndrome boy who was over sixteen when we placed him with Bridgid and Joe. Joe loved other children, Bridgid wanted a larger family and Len was 'daft enough not to be bothered by a daft brother,' she said. All was well for a few weeks and Len made the kind of spectacular progress we had come to expect from this family; but then he began to hit Joe hard on the head whenever Bridgid was not there to stop him and since Joe could not defend himself Len had to go. But by this time Len had been introduced to a religious community which offered care to severely mentally handicapped young people on a one-to-one basis: one worker to each child. Len went to stay with the community to give him and Bridgid and Joe a break from each other but it clearly suited him better than a family and he stayed on. In due course he was christened and Bridgid became his godmother. Had there been time one of the community would have adopted him before he was eighteen.

We would not have thought of looking for a community instead of a family for Len. But if we accept that single parents are normal families, should we not also be looking at people who have other life styles? And Len's community offers as stable, as warm and as permanent a home background as any we have come across. It is not an institution, it is not a Home set up for one particular group of people by another, it is a community of people who choose to live together and to share their lives with handicapped people. There are other communities, other groupings, which may be interested or already involved in shared child care, but have never thought of adoption. The law says that only a single person or two people married to each other can adopt a child, but the care and responsibility could be shared by many.

Isla and Zita might have settled with a group of people who shared their background and interests. They were black sisters around school leaving age, and they soon made up their minds that families were not for them. They wanted security, they wanted to live with black people, they wanted to belong to somebody after fifteen years in care, but not to a mother and father and sisters and brothers. They did not want to have to break into a tight family circle, but they might have welcomed the idea of a caring commune if we had been able to find one, or indeed if we had known where and how to look.

We have never been approached by a group of people who wanted to adopt a child, but perhaps we have not reached people who live in groups, or if we have reached them we have not encouraged them to consider themselves as an adoptive family. Not a straight two parent family or a more unusual one parent family but a group of women or of men or of women and men together, who want to include children in their lives and who can offer children a different kind of family experience. At a time when more and more young people are experimenting with different ways of living together and when traditional families are becoming less and less permanent, it is appropriate that we should look for alternatives to family placement. Or perhaps we should be looking for alternative families.

19   The Lessons Learnt

We continually try to make a meaningful whole out of all the bits and pieces we have learnt: bits about children and pieces about families. If we put them together, will they help us to know who will make good parents, which children will be hardest to place and what will be a problem? We have agonised beforehand over one particular aspect of a placement only to be confounded later by something quite different. We worried about how on earth we would place Hugh who needed a kidney machine, but we placed him in record time, while a relatively ordinary little boy stuck for much longer. We have tried to make sense of our experience so far, to help ourselves and the people who want to adopt to reach better decisions more quickly.

Once we got as far as making a check list of negative family signals. Clearly there were linking factors between one disruption and another and we wanted to create an early warning system. It was a frustrating task. Each suggestion any one of us made was countered by the other three with examples of families who said or did or were exactly that and yet had gone on to a successful adoption. Finally we put down six points and we agreed that if three of them were combined we should sound the alarm. The list has been useful. It has reminded us of topics to discuss with families, and it has helped us to be wise with hindsight when a placement or an introduction has not worked out. 'Look' we have said, 'a, b and c applied: one partner had an extreme attitude to authority, either too respectful or too confronting, the other partner would not talk about himself either out of reticence or out of arrogance and there were misunderstandings with us which could have indicated their mixed feelings about adoption.' They could, but they need not have done. Misunderstandings occur within the best regulated adoption agencies. The man's reluctance to speak could have been well balanced by the woman's readiness and her fights with authority could have seemed only too well founded at the time. We appreciate parents who can make a nuisance of themselves for their child's sake. Similarly inflexibility may be interpreted as steadfastness when a placement works and as rigidity when it does not. Extreme eccentricity may be creative if it engages the child, but it could be sinister if the child finds it distasteful. And the last danger signal on the list is as often the telling factor in success as it is in failure.

If parents do not agree about their child to be, if they see the child from different viewpoints, they could be heading for trouble because they will not be able to handle the child consistently and the child will be able to play one off against the other. Or they could be establishing themselves as two independent, confident adults who can pool their resources and complement each other in order to parent a child. So we have learnt that what we learn can only help us to consider an ever wider range of possibilities and that we will never be able to produce a blueprint for success.

We have even had to redefine our expectations of success. A successful placement, we had anticipated, would be one where parents and children come to grips with the difficulties and sort them out. But we know that some families never come to grips with the difficulties, they live side by side with them, sometimes evading them, sometimes not seeing they are there and they are not less successful than the families who confront. Among biological parents there are also those parents who actively bring up their children and those who let their children grow up with them. And the success or otherwise of placing older and handicapped children cannot be measured in terms of adoption orders made by the court. A seemingly smooth placement may erupt two years after legal adoption or even later, but then a tempestuous adolescence may be the norm for children growing up in a particular family.

One boy we placed when he was fifteen left home when he was sixteen and did not even keep in touch with his parents.

He was in Borstal by the time he was eighteen. He wrote to his parents from Borstal and asked to come home. They visited him every week until he was released. He is home now and his parents are hopeful that the placement is at last beginning to be a success.

We do not know what will happen in adolescence to those handicapped children adopted in infancy. Will Jill and Susie and Ben be as rewarding for their families when they are mentally handicapped young adults? If Robin becomes un-manageable at home and has to go back into residential care will that make the adoption any less worthwhile? Should we not encourage and enable the adoptive parents of disabled children to make whatever arrangements they think suitable, even if this occasionally means some kind of placement away from home? The child would still have parents to fight for the best, to make the arrangements, to monitor progress and maintain a relationship. Natural parents, reluctantly and sadly have to separate from some of their children for some of the time and when children grow up it is right that they should make their home elsewhere. There is no reason why adoptive parents of disabled children should feel that they have to do more for ever.

The mother of Edward, the tall boy, has brought up a Down's sydrome son of her own. She taught him to read and write and guided him towards becoming the socially competent and delightful young man he now is. But she also planned for his future and persevered until she found what he needed. When he became an adult, later than her other sons, he went to live in a village community to learn independence and a trade. He has become a member of that community and comes home for holidays and Christmas like all the other children of the family who are grown up. His mother is now thinking of adopting a Down's syndrome boy and we would be glad if she could make the same arrangements for him.

Even if a placement does finally disrupt we have learnt to regard the disruption as a painful step towards another successful placement. The British Agencies for Adoption and Fostering offers a thought-provoking service to agencies with a disruption on their hands and we have used it gratefully. BAAF will convene and chair a meeting attended by the adopters who have had to give up, the adoption agency staff and the local authority workers in order to reconsider what is known of the child's history and to re-examine the process leading up to placement and its disruption. We have to find out whether we misunderstood the circumstances, or the circumstances changed, or we took an unjustified risk. Thus Ben's parents, who had also wanted to adopt Hope, were able to get their own sense of failure into perspective alongside ours and the local authority's, for it became clear that none of us had really known the child we placed.

Hope's biological parents had not been able to accept a Down's syndrome child and she was left in hospital and received into care. She had had two foster home breakdowns and was living in a subnormality hospital when she was referred to us and she was still only four years old. Instead of pausing to try to understand this little girl's complicated personality, we rushed in to rescue her and we had to stop and do our learning later during the weeks of distress and at the disruption meeting.

We had concentrated too much on the effect Hope might have on a stable family unit, and particularly on Ben, the little Down's syndrome boy who was younger than Hope and had also had too many moves. But we had not reckoned with the impact Ben would have on Hope who had spent a year in a hospital ward in which she was the only moving, walking child. The others had been ranged in a variety of cots and beds all round the wall. Hope went stiff with fear and set up a plaintive wail whenever Ben was in the same room with her. He was a rollicking, noisy child and the greater Hope's reaction, the more he provoked her. Life with both children was hardly possible and it got worse.

Only when the parents finally gave themselves permission to let go could they act decisively like the good parents they are. They agreed to become Hope's foster parents until another family was found. They separated the two children as much as was practical and were able to restrain Ben and protect Hope more competently when they felt they were giving a short term service and not serving a life sentence. They managed to get Hope used to other children, although she could never get used to Ben. They got to know her well enough to introduce her to her next parents.

When Hope moved she went to a busy family with five other children but not one of them like Ben. She is still a complex little character, but she has been absorbed into this easy going family. She has been nursed through serious illnesses, proved herself a survivor and she will never go back to a subnormality hospital. We cannot know whether it would have worked as well if we had not got it wrong the first time and been given the chance to learn from our mistakes.

We learned different lessons from Ernie's failed introductions to one family followed by a placement with another and then a disruption. Ernie was the fourteen-year-old with an adult body and a younger mind who had ground down the confidence of one family and physically terrorised his single parent in his determination to get back to his Children's Home and the only parent figure he wanted: his housemother who had looked after him for nine years.

The work with Ernie taught us to examine more carefully how much an older child can be expected to put into a placement that is going to change his life. We had already learnt that institutionalised teenage children with a multiplicity of handicaps are not likely to make the necessary investment to make the change work. We knew from Doris and from Isla and Zita that adolescents can make their own decisions about families, but Ernie taught us that older children capable of making a commitment and apparently deciding to make one may sabotage their own plans because they have a real attachment elsewhere which has not been acknowledged and which they do not understand. After the disruption meeting when we told Ernie that we would not be finding him another family he became more upset than we had ever seen him. He thought we were telling him that he was not good enough to have parents. We had to work on it to help him understand that it was all right not to want to have parents.

Doris, Isla and Zita and Ernie are black. We have learnt lessons working with them. We do not know whether we should have learnt that all four of them might be with families now if we could have offered them black ones.

We have learnt to put in more background work before we begin to find parents for children. We have learnt to invite the local authority social workers or foster parents to Parents for Children even before we meet the child. We have learnt to show the way we work and to share our optimism as well as our reservations from the very beginning to counter any suspicion about our unorthodox methods. We have even learnt to answer civilly when an adoption officer from a local authority wants to know whether we take up adopters' references as required by law. We have learnt to accept that local authority social workers and their seniors can be out of the office and away on holiday at the same time and that if work has to come to a standstill during their absence because a decision has to be made, it can be made when they return. We have learnt to appreciate that frantic social workers, if we communicate the need, will somehow manage to do the impossible for a child in their care. We have learnt that if a third party is involved when a child is at boarding school, in hospital or in a special Home belonging to a voluntary agency then the work becomes three times as complicated. Three times as much background preparation will have to be put in so that we can all begin from the same starting point, for it is unlikely that the local authority and the third party will have had the time to prepare each other.

We have learnt to value the policy meeting we hold when we are about to start work with a child. We have tried to update it and improve it and fashion it as the basic tool for working together with a local authority to place a child for adoption. The policy meeting offers an opportunity for everyone who holds responsibility for the placement to make their claim, state their terms, voice their doubts, make conditions and stipulations, share their resources and define their roles. The meeting confirms the aims, plans the process and assigns responsibility for preparation, family finding, introductions, placement and post placement support. The notes of the meeting are in the child's file for prospective families to read and they say that they find it reassuring to see that so much thought from so many people has gone into planning for their child.

On the other hand and at the other end where they live,

parents have told us that the difficulties of adoption do not lie with the child but with social workers, doctors, teachers, health visitors and the housing department and the Department of Health and Social Security. Families can be inundated with well meaning professional visitors who overlap their briefs so that a new blind toddler could have six callers in one week.

The school nurse, the health visitor, the local authority adoption officer and the psychologist from the education department wanting to do a domiciliary assessment, as well as the Parents for Children worker, may follow each other hot foot and then spend much time finding out what the other five are doing and have said. And this is without any of the supporting people the family might choose to invite, like their own friends and relations, other parents of blind children or specialists from local voluntary agencies.

We have learnt that such confusion for families and frustration for workers can be avoided by a meeting of interested parties just before the blind toddler is placed for adoption. No one wants to do the work that someone else is already doing, but many of our placements raise the anxiety of caring professionals who want to be assured that every foreseeable possibility, eventuality and risk is being covered by someone.

The Department of Health and Social Security does not want to be unnecessarily inquisitorial with a single parent about to adopt a severely retarded son nor does the housing department want to penalise a mother who needs to move because her new child is in a wheelchair, but the officials concerned cannot be expected to comprehend this kind of situation unless we take the trouble to explain it beforehand. Pressurised administrators are just not used to young women who deliberately make themselves handicapped by becoming the parents of disabled children. Even the GP may look askance and the school may persist in calling the parent a foster mother because that is more usual and the court and its appointed officers may behave as though they were being asked to adopt the troublesome child themselves.

We have a lot of explaining to do and even then we may not be heard. We were not able to avoid the most humiliating interview for one woman who claimed supplementary benefit in order to stay at home with her disabled son nor were we able to protect one couple from the most crass questioning by an inexperienced court officer who had never before acted as Guardian ad Litem in an adoption and was hoping to practise on a totally unconventional family which has adopted a bevy of hard to place children and is inexplicably ready to adopt one more.

We have tried to learn as we have gone along about second and third placements and even fourth, fifth and sixth placements. Adopting another child with special needs is not the same as having another biological child, just as adoption is not the same as giving birth. We have not learnt enough and are struggling not to fall between two stools. We do not want to make parents who have done it once feel that they have to start again at the beginning, but at the same time we do not want to offer a second class service to them or to the child.

Josephine's mother and father, who had already reared seven children, worked harder and travelled further to prepare for their multiply disabled daughter than most parents. Now they are doing the same for Sheeraz who has similar handicaps, but is an entirely different child. Whereas Josephine was tough, Sheeraz is frail; whereas Josephine was shut off and pulled away from the unknown because she went blind when she was nine months old, Sheeraz was born blind and is unafraid of new objects and is eager to explore her surroundings. Whereas Josephine had been loved as a small normal baby, Sheeraz spent the first year of her life in hospital in acute discomfort, immobile, held by foam rubber shaped to her body.

At least Sheeraz is younger than Josephine and if she joins the family a natural order will prevail, but Geoffrey aged eight was adopted after his baby brother and his parents had never lived with a child of over two years of age. They had to prepare for an older child and they had to prepare for Geoffrey who was a very particular older child, but even then, they said afterwards, they had not been prepared for the different ways they would respond to their two children. They had fallen in love with their baby, their first, the moment they saw him in the nursery at the Children's Home. He had been sick and was undersized and they were besotted by him. They never faltered in their commitment to Geoffrey a year later but they had to work harder to get to know him so that they could love him too. Natural parents also feel differently about each of their biological children because each one is different, but it is easier when they all start off at the same age. The national disruption rate for second placements is higher than the disruption rate for first placements and since our own experience has followed this trend we need to learn more.

It has been rewarding to learn that older children can be healed by younger children. We started out with a conviction that children need not be adopted as the youngest in a family but this was fairly new thinking and we had little experience to base it on. We have been moved many times by the unquestioning acceptance and instinctive compassion young home-grown children have shown towards older adopted ones, who in turn have responded to these simple overtures with unforeseen tenderness.

Danny, at fourteen, was the older brother many four- and five-year-olds wish they could have to take them to watch football and to buy sweets. For Danny, the little brothers were not the threatening rivals older boys would have been and if the parents went out and left Danny in charge for an hour, they invariably found Danny on the floor when they got back, grinning sheepishly, being a train or a car or a horse, with the two little boys jumping all over him.

Dawn reacted with loyalty and affection to the eight-year-old brother who opened ranks to welcome her into the family and who greeted her with gladness whenever she came home. Hannah came to life through her little sister. Sixteen-year-old Marion and ten-year-old Ruth have forged a relationship which gives joy to their parents and one younger home-grown daughter is helping her older adopted brother through the scares and hurts of parents who have begun to fight. Families have described the bonds between their younger children and their new older child as the bonus of the adoption.

There appears to be no best order to build a family by adoption but as adopters have a choice which purely biological families do not have, it is only right that they should use it. Some families only feel comfortable if they add children in order of age. Some families like to keep home grown children as the youngest and the oldest and they slot adopted children into the middle. Some families like to start in the middle and keep adding an adopted child at the top and a home-grown one at the bottom. Some families take the children who need them most and fit them in whatever age they are.

A few of the bits we learn are like pieces of a jigsaw which do not look as though they fit in anywhere but they do. Like the piece about moving. Nearly all our families have moved once and some twice or even three times since we have known them. They have changed houses, changed jobs and changed careers with hardly any upheaval. Traditionally adopters are supposed to be stable families who put down deep roots and stick to their employment. We know that the population on the whole is becoming more mobile but the mobility of our adopters is beyond the norm. We are astonished when families planning to adopt a child with special needs plan to move at the same time. Or when the wage earner decides to stop earning and go to college and live on a grant just as the child is being placed. Because we could not contemplate such a combination of changes in our own lives, we are amazed that others can, but we are not adopting and they are. Families have to be able to make an investment in change to adopt a 'hard to place' child and the extent of the change cannot be circumscribed. Unusual mobility should perhaps be equated with unusual flexibility.

We said: 'no forms' to keep us flexible but we have learnt that we need some forms though only a small fraction of what is generally thought necessary. Quite recently we took on a disabled baby and the referring local authority was still trying to catch up with its forms two months after we had placed the child with her new family in the local authority's own area.

One of the most vital pieces in our jigsaw has been to learn that everyone works to different time scales and different rhythms and that we speed families up or slow children down at our peril. There is no average time it takes to place a child; we have done it in two months and we have taken two years. There is no ideal timing for introductions and there is no way a family can do more than they are ready to do.

It is no good presenting new parents with a whole list of

things they have to do for their new child. James needed to see an eye specialist, an ear, nose and throat specialist, a plastic surgeon and a developmental consultant. James' previous hospital caretakers were alarmed because the Deightons did not do everything at once just as the hospital would have done it. They did what was immediately necessary. They had his eyes tested and his ears syringed but without much enthusiasm because it took months of making James their own before they could feel that necessity. In their own good time they are doing more for James than anyone expected could be done, but they are not following a medical schedule, they are seeing to the needs of their son. James is about to have further surgery for his ears so that they will support glasses which in turn will help his sight.

One piece of the jigsaw turns up regularly to make us take another look at the picture: five families are no better than one if it is the right one. There is nothing to be gained from the numbers game in adoption. We are pleased and excited when we have a good response to publicity for a child, but we have as often placed a child successfully when only one family has shown interest. We are also happy of course if we place more than our average number of children in a year, but if we place fewer because they are older and more handicapped then we must settle for having done something different rather than more of it. Single parents, we have learnt, also defy the numbers game.

One parent families are not half two parent families. Single mothers and fathers do not perform only half the parenting that couples manage, nor do they have to compensate their child for the missing partner. Parents on their own are offering something couples do not have to give for they do not have to balance the claim of husband or wife or resident lover with those of the adopted child and for some children this is more important than two parents. We know children need good models of both sexes and that they need to observe good relationships between women and men but the models need not necessarily be only their parents.

Children make demands on parents and so do we. We have learnt that it is helpful for adopters to be asked to work hard during preparation and to travel over long distances and to rearrange their timetable to suit the child during introductions because our demands are as nothing compared to those the child will make on their time, their capacities and their emotions. If families cannot manage the demanding early stages of adoption they are not going to cope with the rigours of taking a child. We have learnt that it will not work if we have to do all the running for people who want to adopt. If we find out about schools, hospitals, local parent groups and specialist provision it will not help families to search for the next service they will need. If we take on all the burden of travelling and work entirely in the evenings and at weekends because the family has no transport and cannot take time off work it does not augur well for their life with a handicapped or an unpredictable child.

We do not expect families to put jobs at risk or to prove themselves by journeying, but we do want them to take responsibility for becoming parents and that will mean making a response to some pretty unusual demands. Clearly not all parents can travel, not everybody can take time off work and not every family can negotiate the system the way we have learnt to do and they make good enough adopters nevertheless. We do travel far and we do much of our thinking in the car or reading on long train journeys; we do work evenings and weekends but we have also learnt that part of giving an adoption service is to make reasonable demands.

It is unreasonable, we have learnt, to expect that each one of us could work with any child or with any family. There is no complicated system of choosing or allocating and generally we take the next child on the list when we have a space and we share the families out among us. But we can say, 'I would rather not,' and no one will dissuade us because we have to speak for the child or for the family and we will not do them justice if we are not in sympathy with them.

Parents may also feel that they cannot get on with one of us and we hope they will say so, but we cannot know if they always do. In the beginning we thought it was important for the child's worker to work with the families for that child. We learned that the parents have a better service if they do not feel pressurised by the child's needs while they are still exploring what they have to offer. It is too easy for the child's worker to make parents feel either that they must rescue the child or that no one is good enough for this particular child. We now have a separate worker for the parents and that worker remains with the family and gets to know the child in placement if they proceed.

So the bits and pieces do make a picture, but we discovered early on that we need help to see it. We need consultants and advisers and our adoption panel to help us digest what we learn. Our practice and policy consultant joins the team meeting once a month to help us look at agency functioning and every two weeks our team consultant helps us to look at the way we work together, at what is helpful and what gets in the way of decision making. We retain a legal adviser and we have a weekly session with our medical adviser to discuss the implication of medical reports for each child and family. Other experts are available if we need them to help us learn about a child's need or a family's capacity and all of them help us to see and to use what we have learnt.

We have certainly used what we have learnt about the likes and dislikes of adoptive families. Many like social occasions and some like occasions when they can get together and talk about issues that concern them but they are not keen on mixing the two. So four times a year we offer workshops to families around topics they have chosen and once a year we organise a picnic for parents and children and friends and relatives and a host of helpers. The sun has regularly helped, too, and there is archery organised by Geoffrey's father; there are games and inflatables and a true banquet created from the pies and cakes and fruit and meats and pastries and flans and salads which the families bring and lay out and share. Every year there are more families and there is more food. It is a happy day for all of us.

We tried to do something like it at Christmas. It was as great a let down as the picnic is an annual delight. Families came because they felt they should when they had better things to do at home. Children were either crabby with anticipation or overfed and tired out with celebration. We gave up and decided that Christmas was a time for families but that the families had better stay at home.

20   The Judge and Father Christmas

'Where will I be at Christmas?' Not only James wants to know. Christmas, whatever else it is, is a time for families. We may all joke about the family reunion when the annual feasting and fighting is done but it is our family to joke about.

Sisters and brothers who hardly speak to each other throughout the year meet at home at Christmas. Parents who are not close to their adult sons and daughters expect them home for Christmas and gentle pressure builds up weeks before as decisions have to be made about who goes where, when, and takes what. Her parents on Christmas Day, his on Boxing Day; it is almost impossible for a young couple to spend Christmas alone and even when they have children of their own they trail all over the country and sleep on floors to fit into the Christmas image of family gatherings.

I know one family with teenage sons who longed to spend Christmas in their own home but they could never find an acceptable excuse for their traditional parents, until they got themselves a cow and had to stay behind to milk it because all the helpful friends and neighbours they knew had gone away as usual.

It is almost unthinkable for a single person to spend Christmas with friends by choice. 'What about your family?' 'Why can't you come home like everyone else?' is the pained re-action and any other conduct threatens to become almost a denial of kith and kin.

How then do children feel who have no families and who live in the midst of mounting Christmas fever from the end of October? Children who are exploited by advertisements: buy this for Dad, and this for Mum, and ask your Uncle to buy so and so; and who see an ever increasing number of sentimental films in which all comes right because it is Christmas. No wonder then that James and others ask, 'Where will I be at Christmas?'

Some residential workers will take children in care to their own homes. Some children will be invited by local families who have befriended them but most will stay in the Children's Home for Christmas with staff who will be on duty and paid to look after them.

'Don't have a child for Christmas, have a child for life.' We put a poster with that kind of message in our shop front window every December. Families are easily moved to offer a strange child a home for Christmas but these children do not need treats; there are plenty of treats in Children's Homes and perhaps even more toys and goodies than most families can afford. The Christmas Sandra spent in the Home, she told us challengingly, was the best she had ever had.

There was turkey and ham and pork with every kind of trimming and pudding and cake and pies and you could choose or have them all. The children had expensive presents: Sandra had a transistor radio and roller skates, only one was broken and the other lost before the end of the holiday. They had crackers and decorations and sweets and fruit and nuts and went out to see the Ice Show and the pantomime and watched colour television as much as they wanted.

A family at Christmas could not have surrounded Sandra with more things and she would not have known what to do with offers of warmth and caring and sharing – on a temporary basis. At least in the Children's Home she was one of the gang; in the family home she would have been and felt the odd one out. It is unfair as well as harmful to tantalise a child with something that is not hers to take but only hers to sample on someone else's terms. So do not have a child for Christmas, but when children come to families for life, Christmas can be a strange and trying time.

Edward's first Christmas was a disaster. No matter how hard his grown up brothers and sister tried to encourage him he would not buy any presents. He was quite ready with a list of his own requirements but he resisted even suggestions to make Christmas cards, something he could have done very well. At fifteen he was too old to be taken bodily to do his

Christmas chores, so nothing was done and his remarkably patient widowed mother let him be. While the rest of the family cleaned and cooked and bought and wrapped, Edward spread his great length out on the floor and got in everybody's way. Rather late he suddenly went off to buy presents for his natural younger brother, who was being adopted elsewhere, and for his Gran, with both of whom he keeps in touch. He spent all the money he had on them, thereby making quite sure that there was nothing else he could buy. It took him forever to wrap the two presents and to post them. He used all the available space and paper to do it and infuriated everybody by using up all of the sellotape. It seemed as though he had never sent a parcel before. When Edward came back from the Post Office he lay down exhausted and waited for Christmas.

By Christmas Eve the rest of the family just could not bear the thought that Edward would have nothing to give. So they bought a big box of chocolates and explained that it was for him to hand round and it could be his present for them. He had to be reminded on Christmas Day, but he dutifully went to his room to collect the chocolates and brought them out and opened them and spilled them all on the floor. His sister, brothers and mother had to scrabble for the Christmas present he did not want to give.

In the end the family was relieved that Edward chose to spend most of the festive season in his own room with his presents. He said he had a lovely Christmas. He hung up his stocking and it was filled. He ate well and liked the wine. He got what he asked for and more.

Much later when we talked about it again he said he thought next Christmas he would buy presents for all the family. That was all. No other comment, no explanation. In fifteen years Edward had lived in ten houses and gone to eleven schools. At Christmas he had learnt to make a list of things he wanted. But the presents Edward hoarded in his room all got broken or inexplicably lost, just like Sandra's. Only in Sandra's Children's Home it didn't really matter and Edward's family minded about the carefully chosen gifts he could not value. We do not know what was expected of Edward in his ten different homes. We do know that he does not value himself and cannot give anything of himself to anybody; and Christmas presents are not that important in comparison, for Christmas comes but once a year, as his family wisely observed.

Not all children are quite as unresponsive to the Christmas spirit as Edward. Sixteen-year-old Hugh went to the other extreme and bought his new father a silver watch and his new mother expensive presents with all the money in his savings bank; quite embarrassing for them and for the other children who gave the soaps and bathsalts and shaving sticks which were more in keeping with family tradition. If you want to give, how do you know what it is right to give?

Nick, who drank the milk, sent his grandmother a card and put a pound in with it. He said: 'Well Nana's very special, isn't she?' How could he know that grandparents send pound notes to grandchildren and that it is not quite the same the other way round? But Nick got it right for his Mum and Dad. He bought a gingerbread heart and asked the baker to write on it in yellow icing sugar: 'To Mum and Dad from Son'. His Mum and Dad will never eat that gingerbread and it hangs in the sitting room with all the other treasured bric-a-brac.

Christmas is a time for families and for observing intricate networks of family traditions. New children have a lot of catching up to do with family rules and rituals for everyday use and they are not likely to take in Christmas specials at the first try. One family I know has a very personal collection of Christmas Tree decorations. Each piece marks an event in the family going back fifty years and their children delight in the stories they all know off by heart; how long would it take a child to get to know them if she did not learn them, literally, at her mother's knee?

All families have their very own Christmas stories when they remember what happened in other years, and every family makes its unique arrangements for the way it celebrates. A child may be so anxious to get things right, he may not even be able to listen to what he is told. James, when he joined his forever family, was involved in every bit of preparation and everything was carefully explained at least twice over, but on the longed for day he was overcome with confusion and could hardly manage to open a present or eat any dinner. When he went to bed that night he wanted to know if Christmas had really been and if it was over.

Some family traditions can be passed on as a gift. Nick's mother remembered that the best part of her childhood Christmasses had been her own mother reading from a book of Christmas verse. She found a copy of the same book and read it to Nick on Christmas morning and he felt pride to be the carrier of a tradition which linked him with his parents' past.

But Geoffrey was bewildered by the tradition in his new family of buying presents for the many cats. He bought some too, and wrapped them solemnly because he very much wanted to fit in. Then he worried. And finally he asked a visitor. He needed to know how the cats were going to find their presents and how they were going to open them.

Hannah has already added to her family's tradition. Her first Christmas was almost as negative as Edward's but when she opened her eyes on her second Christmas morning at home she asked, 'Where's grandma?' even before she thought of presents, because grandma had arrived late on Christmas Eve when Hannah was in bed and she had grown to love her grandma. 'Where's grandma?' say all the family at Christmas now when they mean 'I love you too'.

Peter, the ten-year-old Down's syndrome boy, was excited when he was taken to a store by his single mother to meet Father Christmas. He was amazed by the large, jolly man who sat him on his knee and asked him whether he was a good boy. He was delighted when the jolly red man gave him a toy car, for Peter collects toy cars. Peter in fact collects all sorts of things now and he is learning to read and write and he can knit and sew better than most children of his age and he can ride a bicycle with the best of them. He could not do any of these things when he came but his mother can see no reason why Peter should not be taught many more skills.

Two days after seeing Father Christmas, Peter was excited again because he and his mother and grandmother and aunt went to court for his adoption. Peter was overjoyed when the bewhiskered elderly judge also took him on his knee and asked him if he was a good boy. Peter has become a secure, good natured child in his family and he did not even mind too much when the judge did not give him a present. At least he knew where he would be at Christmas.

Postscript: Where Do We Go From Here?

On the whole we still believe that small works well. We have been tempted to grow but have found excuses to prevent it. Our premises limit expansion and we are unlikely to find a bigger place which would serve families as comfortably. 222 Camden High Street is two minutes from the underground, within easy and direct reach of all mainline railway stations and on twelve bus routes. So where do we go from here? Do we breathe in to accommodate new projects, do we stand still as we are, do we move and spread or do we burst?

We have tried to reassess our role as a voluntary specialist adoption agency. Several years ago we were the first of a few and now there are many and most local authorities are doing some of the same work. There seems no point in becoming bigger in order to place more children, but it seems there is still room for a pioneering agency willing to experiment with policy and practice and prepared to test out 'which children are adoptable' and 'what is a family?'

We know that the children referred to us will be harder and harder to place and that the families we find may be less and less conventional. We are aware that there are other children like Hope and Adam in hospital and welcome working with local authorities and medical staff to find families for them. We hope to be able to attract more alternative families to adopt. We have considered whether we should change our aims in order to find permanent substitute families rather than limit our search to adopters and we have decided that we should continue to follow our first brief because part of our work must be to say clearly and loudly and why we cannot find a parent to adopt a certain child.

At the same time we would like the opportunity to explore

further the idea of 'bridging families': families who can offer a child a bridge between one family and the next or between an institution and parents. We have used bridging families when a placement has not worked and there has had to be a pause before another adoptive family could be found. It always seems better for children to go on than to go back. A bridging family can help a child to understand what has happened and to prepare for the next time, perhaps better than the staff of the Children's Home who could, rightly, feel both resentful about the past and apprehensive about the future.

Once we used a bridging family to help a child who seemed too stuck to make the move to parents. Nick's bridging family gave him the stability and experience of family life he needed and could not get at his understaffed Children's Home where he was the youngest of several disillusioned delinquent adolescents. Other children we have placed would have done better with a bridge in between and we would like to use bridging families to assess and prepare children who are living in hospital when they are referred to us for adoption.

We are not really afraid that we will go on forever doing more and more of the same. As each child is different so is each family and so is the whole adoption process. We are more concerned to find new methods to handle new situations and so improve the quality of the work, than we are to have more bodies to deal with the quantity. We appreciate the seconded adoption workers who come once a year for six months from a local authority and make us explain ourselves and give us their time and energy and exchange ideas with us. We have been unbelievably fortunate in raising money to fund special projects to test out some of those ideas. Unbelievable to us because we had all worked in settings where ideas and projects most often remained pipe dreams or became bees in bonnets.

We have completed a year's project with a psychologist who was attached to us for one day a week. Irene Harris helped us to identify those children whose behaviour would need to be 'translated' from Children's Home to family and she worked with residential staff and parents before, during and after the move. In this way a fourteen-year-old boy was motivated to attain the degree of independence the family expected from him and a four-year-old was trained to sleep through the night before placement and to maintain this pattern afterwards.

Josephine's parents were helped to disentangle one goal from all the others. If Josephine with her multiple disabilities could learn to walk, progress in all directions would follow. It took three months of discipline and ingenuity before Josephine could let go and move forward on her own. She goes on making progress in all directions.

Irene enabled us to look at children differently and to see what we had overlooked. We hope in future to have a permanent, one day a week psychologist; she will not squeeze us out of our working space because, like Irene, most of her time will be spent where the children and families are.

While I have been writing this book Parents for Children has embarked on another project of which we have high expectations. As we have placed more severely disabled children, we have become more perplexed about the kind of support, relief or respite these new families will need. Catherine Macaskill, who has already researched this field, is spending six months with us to find out what families say they want, what professionals say they need and what is available. If the gaps and the discrepancies are exposed we shall want to start more special projects to deal with them.

We have often wished for an all-purpose Parents for Children therapist. Someone to work with parents, with children and with families around such issues as severe learning problems, persistent behaviour problems and marital problems brought to the fore by adoption. On the other hand we do not want to be seen as an agency offering treatment because we work with people's strength and health and do not seek out weaknesses and pathology. It is this which makes adoption work different from other branches of social work and we value it and want to keep it that way. We do not, however, want to ignore the need for therapeutic help and hope to be able to persuade some therapists and psychiatrists, from all over the country, to declare an interest in the issues raised by adoption and perhaps to form a mutually supportive group of practitioners which could be approached by adopters, adoptees and adoption agencies.

The only kind of expansion we have seriously contemplated is a neighbourhood post-adoption service for families grouped together in a geographical area. So far we have not achieved it because, whenever we have identified a cluster of families, we have not found a suitable outside worker locally, or when we have found a willing and able worker, there have not been enough families in the vicinity to set up a separate service. It is still something we think about for the future because, as we grow in years and the families grow in number, it is the post adoption support we give which might make us finally burst unless we find another way.

One other way is for families to get together to offer each other more than we can. National organisations for adoptive, disabled and mixed race families have local branches and there are other specialist parent groups which families have found more suited to their needs than an adoption worker.

Jean and Dick and their two Down's syndrome daughters had the best support from their Parent Teacher Association and the best advice from their local Down's Syndrome Association. Fay's parents founded a new Down's Syndrome Association in their area when they found there was not one. Josephine's parents who will also be Sheeraz' parents are searching out other families with blind children in their county so that they can get together to survey the need and the provision for the future. Some Parents for Children one parent families have formed a mutual support association and some Parents for Children adopters have organised a residential weekend for shared study and leisure.

There are aspects of our work we would like to have more time to develop, Hilary has a talent for making things and we need more materials for our work with children and parents. We have good video equipment and do make video recordings of children we want to place, but the medium has other uses we have not explored. We would like to be better window dressers, be more expert at public relations and write more about the work we do. All these activities would, no doubt, illustrate and enliven our work, but in order to carry them out with any consistency we would almost certainly have to stop placing children. So we will increasingly have to seek help from others who have the time and the expertise and who would be interested enough to work for us on a sessional basis.

As Parents for Children has become established so have we become aware that we have a voice and moreover some responsibility to use it. Policy decisions are made by the Executive Committee, but because the agency is so small and because management and staff work so closely together, we all represent what the agency stands for. There are choices to make about what to support, put weight behind, align with, fight for, hold aloof from and speak out against. It is easy to approve of the 1976 Children Act and to lobby for the enactment of the various clauses which take heed of the best interests of the child.

It is rewarding to be able to launch an idea and to be listened to and consulted. For example, there is our current campaign for children in care to have day books, diaries, memory books or whatever name fits the compilation of a parental memory by the people who are standing in for the parents. A book to hold the childhood that is not recorded in the files.

It is self evident that we do not wish to see the social services and the health services cut by any government. It is logical that we should be members of Harmony, an association for multi-racial and multicultural families. PPIAS, an association of adoptive parents, Mencap, the national association for mentally handicapped people, RADAR, the national association for physically handicapped people and Mind, the national association for mental health.

It is most acceptable that we should support groups which work for racial equality, the child in care, one parent families, a better deal for mentally disabled, or better provision for physically handicapped people. We are quite clear that as an agency we should speak out against any form of injustice and discrimination, if and when we meet it during the course of our work. These affiliations are political choices as all choices must be that are concerned with the relationship between the quality of life, the nation's resources, individual rights and national legislation.

We feel quite comfortable that the agency does not have an

opinion about political issues which have nothing directly to do with our work. We may each have strong beliefs about abortion, nuclear energy, the arms race, the Common Market and Ireland, but whatever our political or religious persuasions, we are not accountable for them to the agency any more than the agency is publicly accountable for our private views.

I am writing this book while I am on study leave. We have each been given six months study leave to take in turn after five years' service. It is one of the many rewards we enjoy, one of the many ways we are taken care of. We drew lots to decide the order of our going and our proposals for study had to be agreed. Juliet went first. She spent six months in America observing trends in adoption and the development of agencies on which our own is based. She went away feeling worn out and came back sparkling with interest and eager to share her experiences and her reactions. While she was abroad she met Rick and while I have been writing she has left us again to marry him.

She is the only one of the social work group to leave in the seven years we have been together and it is more than a loss. It has had to be a reformation. We have not even tried to replace Juliet, instead we have reformed the group with a new worker. Someone had to leave first if we were not all to fossilise on the job and perhaps Juliet has opened the door for us.

However closely we work together, and however inter-dependent we become, the agency functions as a team and will go on functioning as a different team whenever workers come and go. We have always tried to give an agency service and although Juliet has gone and is missed, and families and children have a new worker, the service has been, we hope, continuous. Our love goes with Juliet; she is, as we are sadly aware, only our second placement with a single man.

While I have been writing, another of our adoptive families has split up and their adopted handicapped son will have to share his fate with their home-grown daughter. They will both stay with the mother who will become another single parent. Other families will separate and divide as we go ahead to place more children for adoption. We cannot legislate for greater permanence for adopted children than ordinary children are guaranteed. We cannot even promise children a future, we can only offer them the best we know of the present.

While I have been writing, Sandra's fourteen-strong family has grown again. They have found room for Down's syndrome infant twins. Their capacity for taking and giving and loving defies comprehension, but we believe them when they say that all children are a blessing. On the day the twins arrived twelve children aged between seven and seventeen had a variety of ailments to prevent them going to school and the welcome that was lavished on the babies was their introduction to family life.

While I have been writing Sheeraz has become Josephine's sister. As I began this book tentative discussions were going on and now Sheeraz is placed. There were many stages in between. There were opportunities to withdraw but the parents were steadfast if careful. Our adoption panel, and all of us, agonised over whether we were encouraging the family to take on too much, but we agreed in the end that the family has talked and thought more about their ability to absorb another child that we can. So Sheeraz is the seventy-fifth child to be placed for adoption by Parents for Children and, momentous and unique as were the events that led to her placement, we look forward to many as astounding before this book is published.

Families will have their own ideas about Parents for Children. Parents will not view it quite as we do and children will certainly not. We know that colleagues in other agencies and local authorities do not see us as we see ourselves. Sue and Katina, or Phillida, Juliet and Hilary would have written different books; this one is mine, for all of them.

Some Facts about Parents, Children and Parents for Children

THE CHILDREN
75 children were placed by May 1983:

24 were Down's syndrome children:
  16 were aged under 2 years
  3 were aged between 2–5 years
  1 was aged 8
  1 was aged 11
  3 were aged 15 and over

  1 was blind
  5 had serious heart defects

28 were otherwise disabled children:
  9 were aged under 5
  6 were aged 5–10
  12 were aged 10–15
  1 was aged $16\frac{1}{2}$

  6 were mentally handicapped
  6 were physically handicapped
  16 were both mentally and physically handicapped

Disabilities included:
Achondroplasia – abnormality of growth of long bones which results in dwarfing
Acute Epilepsy – interruption of consciousness associated with convulsions
Adrenal Hyperplasia – abnormality of the adrenal gland which affects the control of minerals and hormones
Ascot's Syndrome – association of congenital defects of the facial features and genitalia

Blindness
Brain Damage – damage to the brain due to injury, disease or genetic factors
Cerebral Palsy – brain damage associated with a persistent disorder of movement and posture
Chromosomal Abnormalities – abnormality of that part of the living cell which carries the genes
Cystic Fibrosis – genetic and life threatening disorder of the mucous secreting glands and the sweat glands of the body
Diabetes Insipidus – a rare condition marked by increased flow of urine needing daily injections
Down's Syndrome – chromosomal abnormality characterised by a 'Mongolian' appearance and mental retardation
Hydrocephalus – an abnormal accumulation of fluid within the brain
Meobius Syndrome – weakness of muscles of the face and eyes often combined with limb malformation
Profound Deafness
Spina Bifida – congenital abnormality in the spinal canal associated with paralysis of the lower limbs
Tuberose Sclerosis – genetic, usually fatal abnormality of the brain characterised by mental retardation and epilepsy
Turner's Syndrome – genetically determined short stature, webbed neck, mild mental retardation, congenital heart defect.

23 were normal older children:
    9 were aged between 5–10
  10 were aged between 10–15
    4 were aged over 15

  12 were diagnosed as maladjusted

23 children were placed from foster homes
52 children were placed from residential care

THE PARENTS
56 families had children placed with them by May 1983:
14 were one parent families:
    9 were childless

1 had 13 children
3 were widows and had grown up children
1 was a man
4 gave up work outside the home to adopt
8 were unwaged at the time of placement
6 single parents worked outside the home at time of placement

42 were married couples:
13 were childless
8 had one child
7 had more than 3 children
3 mothers gave up work outside the home to adopt
7 mothers worked outside the home at time of placement
All couples were wage earners at time of placement.

17 families described themselves as religious

24 wage earners worked irregular hours: shift work, own business, working at home.

14 families needed and wanted long term financial assistance

Multiple, second and subsequent placements by Parents for Children:
3 family groups of 3
1 family group of 2
9 second placements
6 children placed with 1 family over 6 years

Placements by other agencies with Parents for Children families:
before PfC placement 9
after PfC placement 18

DISRUPTION
14 placements disrupted by May 1983

2 children disrupted before legal adoption and were replaced in special projects

1 child disrupted before legal adoption and was not replaced

8 children disrupted before legal adoption and were replaced with other families

1 child disrupted after legal adoption and was received into care

2 fifteen- and sixteen-year-old brothers left home a year after placement and did not want another family. The younger returned to the family when he was eighteen

NOT PLACED

13 children were not placed

We could not find parents for 2:
    1 mentally ill, retarded girl of 14
    1 retarded and emotionally disturbed boy of 15

7 older teenagers withdrew or were withdrawn from the adoption plan:
    1 lives in a hostel
    2 are waiting for their own council flats
    1 is remaining in his Children's Home
    1 returned part time to her natural family
    2 are placed in a special project

4 children were withdrawn because the parents PfC found were not accepted by the local authorities

8 children were introduced to more than 1 family before placement

2 children have died in placement

Useful Addresses

BRITISH AGENCIES FOR ADOPTION AND
FOSTERING 11 Southwark Street, London SE1 1RQ
(01 407 8800)

DOWNS CHILDREN'S ASSOCIATION Quinborne Centre,
Ridgacre Road, Birmingham B32 2TW (021 427 1374)

HARMONY (Association of racially mixed families) 22
St Mary's Road, Meare, Glastonbury, Somerset BA6 9SP
(04586 311)

MENCAP (The Royal Society for Mentally Handicapped
Children and Adults) MENCAP National Centre, 123 Golden
Lane, London EC1Y 0RT (01 253 9433)

MIND (National Association for Mental Health) 22 Harley
Street, London W1N 2ED (01 637 0741)

PARENTS FOR CHILDREN 222 Camden High Street,
London NW1 8QR (01 485 7526/48)

PPIAS (Parent to Parent Information on Adoption Services)
Lower Boddington, Daventry, Northamptonshire NN11 6YB
(0327 60295)

RADAR (The Royal Association for Disability and Rehabili-
tation) 25 Mortimer Street, London W1N 8AB
(01 637 5400)

Endpiece

Many people who read this book will never adopt a child with special needs. Some people who will not adopt may want to know whether they can help children with special needs to be adopted.

Parents for Children has to raise one third of its annual income through voluntary grants and donations. Parents for Children also draws on a sponsors fund which is administered by one of the adoptive families and used for the benefit of individual children and parents. Contributions can be sent to Parents for Children at 222 Camden High Street, London NW1 8QR and marked either 'general funds' or 'sponsors fund'.